FAITH OF THE FATHERLESS

FAITH OF THE FATHERLESS
The Psychology of Atheism

PAUL C. VITZ

SPENCE PUBLISHING COMPANY • DALLAS
1999

Published in the United States by
Spence Publishing Company
111 Cole Street
Dallas, Texas 75207

Library of Congress Cataloging-in-Publication Data
for the Hardcover Edition

Vitz, Paul C., 1935-
     Faith of the fatherless : the psychology of atheism / Paul C.
Vitz.
         p. cm.
     Includes bibliographical references (p.   ) and index.
     ISBN 1-890626-12-0 (hardcover)
     1. Atheism–Psychology.   2. Atheists–Psychology Case
studies.   3. Theists–Psychology Case studies.   4. Father and
child–Religious aspects.   I. Title.
     BL2747.3.V58 1999
     211'.8'019—dc21   99-16667

ISBN 1-890626-25-2 (pbk.)

Printed in the United States of America

Dedicated with love to my children
Rebecca, Jessica, Daniel,
Peter, Michael, and Anna

Contents

Preface

ONLY AS IT STARTS TO FADE can we see how strange the modern world has been. It is natural that some distance is needed for the characteristics of the "modern" to become obvious, and nothing has been more typical of public life, especially, than the presumption of atheism. God has been banished from public discourse so thoroughly that in today's high schools we teach about condoms and masturbation, but are legally prohibited from making reference to the Deity.

The rejection of God in our schools is just one small example of the triumph of atheism. That such a rejection of God should have triumphed is quite remarkable—even bizarre. After all, the United States has long been known as a seriously religious country. In the 1840s, Alexis de Tocqueville clearly identified the profoundly religious character of the United States: "America is still the place where the Christian religion has kept the greatest real power over men's souls. . . . The religious atmosphere of the country was the first thing that struck me upon arrival in the United States. . . . Religion, which never intervenes directly in the government of society, should therefore be considered as the first of [America's] political institutions."[1]

James Turner, a historian who has studied the origins of atheism in Western society and in America in particular, has pointed out that "the known unbelievers of Europe and America before the French Revolution [1789] numbered fewer than a dozen or two. For disbelief in God remained scarcely more plausible than disbelief in gravity."[2] America remained more or less an atheist-free nation for many decades into the nineteenth century. Even in intellectual and academic circles, atheism did not become respectable until about 1870, little more than a century ago, and it continued to be restricted to small numbers of intellectuals into the twentieth century.[3] Not until the past half-century has is become a predominant public assumption.

Yet even throughout these last fifty years—which is as long as the Gallup Poll[4] has been asking the question, "Do you believe in God?"—well over 90 percent of Americans have regularly answered, "Yes." Nevertheless, references to God in public discourse have become extremely uncommon; we have become a nation of public and practical atheists. This social condition has been well described by Richard John Neuhaus as the "naked public square."[5]

In the academic world, serious reference to God in scholarly writing—not to mention the use of notions like "providence"—is altogether taboo. Abstract secular concepts such as "progress," "class warfare," "patriarchal society," "self-actualization"—along with other equally ethe-real notions such as "survival of the fittest" and "evolu-tion"—are, however, pervasive and accepted. The situation in the academy is such that to refer to God in any seri-ous way would bring the legitimacy of one's scholarship into question.

In general, historians agree that atheism is a recent and distinctively Western phenomenon and that no other culture has manifested such a widespread public rejection of the divine.[6] In view of the suddenness of the public shift from accepted belief to accepted unbelief, in view of its rarity in the historical record of other cultures, and in view of the continued high prevalence of private be-lief in God, atheism needs to be examined—indeed, ex-plained.

The importance of atheism is, I trust, obvious since it constitutes a major determinant of a person's worldview. For example, if one believes in a personal God, life has obvious meaning, and one generally takes seriously the issues of moral and social responsibility. As Voltaire is reported to have said, "Don't tell the servants there is no God, or they will steal the silver." This view was later shared by Sigmund Freud, who believed that religion was necessary to keep the masses from acting on their sexual and aggressive impulses.[7]

In contrast, the worldview of those who reject God creates problems like the meaninglessness and the alien-ation of modern life that so many report these days. Atheism, of course, has been a central assumption of many modern ideologies and intellectual movements—commu-nism, socialism, much of modern philosophy, most of contemporary psychology, and materialistic science. Indeed, I will take it for granted that atheism is one of the distinctive features of what is meant by the modern.

Now some might say that the reason for the dominance of atheism is that it is true: there *is* no God. I will address some aspects of this question in the last chapter, where I will treat briefly the issue of how to approach the case for belief. For now, let me simply point out that although it may be possible to prove the existence of God, it is clearly impossible to prove the nonexistence of God— since to prove the nonexistence of anything is intrinsically impossible. In other words, atheism is an assumption made by certain people about the nature of the world, and these people have been, in the past century, extraordinarily successful at controlling the acceptable view on the matter. In particular, there seems to be a widespread assumption, throughout much of our intellectual community, that belief in God is based on all kinds of irrational, immature needs and wishes, whereas atheism or skepticism flows from a rational, grown-up, no-nonsense view of things as they really are.

To challenge the *psychology* of this viewpoint is the primary concern of this book.[8] As I present the evidence from the lives of atheists, I will be looking for regularities, for patterns that distinguish their lives from those of a comparable group of theists.

OVER THE YEARS in which this book has been in preparation, many people and several organizations have contributed to the development of my thought on this subject. I offer my sincere thanks to Enrico Cantore, SJ, Edward

Oakes, sj, James Hitchcock, and Joseph Koterski, sj, for their useful comments on early drafts. And most especially I would like to thank Iain T. Benson for his many valuable contributions, especially to the sections on Samuel Butler, H. G. Wells, and Walker Percy.

I am also grateful to the Veritas Forum and Intervarsity Christian Fellowship, which sponsored my lectures on the psychology of atheism at a number of universities, including the University of Florida, the University of Georgia, Ohio State University, Texas A&M University, and the University of Virginia. I have benefited from the many useful comments from students who have heard me speak on those campuses, as well as from members of student organizations at Princeton University, Columbia University, and New York University.

Finally, I owe a great debt of gratitude to my wife, Dr. Evelyn (Timmie) Birge Vitz, whose encouragement and editing were so essential to this project.

FAITH OF THE FATHERLESS

Intense Atheism

I WILL BEGIN by addressing the deep personal psychology of the great—or at least the passionate and influential—atheists. Of course, atheism has not simply been the expression of the personal psychology of important atheists: it has received much support from social, economic, and cultural forces. Nevertheless, atheism began in the personal lives of particular people, many of them the leading intellectuals of the modern period, such as Friedrich Nietzsche, Sigmund Freud, Bertrand Russell, and Jean-Paul Sartre. I propose that atheism of the strong or intense type is to a substantial degree generated by the peculiar psychological needs of its advocates.

But why should one study the psychology of atheists at all? Is there any reason to believe that there are consistent psychological patterns in their lives? Indeed, there is a coherent psychological origin to intense atheism. To begin, it should be noted that self-avowed atheists tend, to a remarkable degree, to be found in a narrow range of social and economic strata: in the university and intellectual world and in certain professions. Today, as a rule, they make up a significant part of the governing class. (By contrast, believers are found much more widely throughout the entire social spectrum.) Given the relatively small numbers of unbelievers and the limited number of social settings in which they are found, there is certainly an a priori reason for expecting regularity in their psychology.

Nevertheless, the reader might ask if this is not unfair—even uncalled for. Why submit atheism to psychological analysis at all? Is this relevant to the issue of unbelief? Here we must remember that *it is atheists themselves who began the psychological approach to the question of belief.* Indeed, many atheists are famous for arguing that believers suffer from illusions, from unconscious and infantile needs, and from other psychological deficits. A significant part of the atheist position has been an aggressive interpretation of religious belief as arising from psychological factors, not the nature of reality. Furthermore, this interpretation has been widely influential. In short, the theory that God is a projection of our own needs is a familiar modern position and is, for example, presented in countless university courses. But the psychological concepts used so effectively to interpret religion by those who reject God are double-edged swords that can also, indeed easily, be used to explain their unbelief.

Finally, a valid reason for exploring the psychology of atheism is to give us some understanding of why certain historical forces common in the modern period have so reliably promoted an atheistic attitude. By identifying psychological factors in the lives of prominent rejectors of God, we will observe how social and economic conditions which fostered a similar psychology also promoted the spread of atheism. By starting with the psychological, we will be able to see how the personal became political. In short, there has been a synchrony between the psychology and the sociology of atheism.

Before beginning, I wish to make two points bearing on the underlying assumptions of the present analysis. First, I assume that the major barriers to belief in God are not rational but can be called, in a general sense, psychological. I am quite convinced that for every person strongly swayed by rational argument, there are countless others more affected by nonrational, psychological factors such as those I will discuss here. One of the earliest theorists of the unconscious, St. Paul, wrote: "I can will what is right, but I cannot do it . . . . I see in my members another law at war with the law of my mind" (Rom. 7:18, 23). Hence, it seems to me sound psychology (as well as sound theology) to accept that psychological factors can be impediments to belief and that these factors are often unconscious. The human heart—no one can truly fathom it or know all its deceits, but it is the proper task of the psychologist at least to try. I propose, then, that irrational, often neurotic, psychological barriers to belief in God are of great importance.

Second, in spite of various difficulties, all of us still have a free choice to accept or reject God. This qualification is not a contradiction of the first. A little elaboration will make this clearer. As a consequence of particular past or present circumstances some may find it much harder to believe in God. But presumably they can still choose to move toward God or to move away. Likewise, those born without psychological barriers to belief can choose either path. Although the ultimate issue is one of the will, it is nonetheless possible to investigate those psychological factors that predispose one to unbelief, that make the path toward God especially difficult.[1]

The Projection Theory of Belief in God[2]

As is generally known, Freud's criticism of belief in God is that such a belief is untrustworthy because of its psychological origins. That is, God is a projection of our own intense, unconscious desires. He is a wish-fulfillment derived from childish needs for protection and security. Since these wishes are largely unconscious, any denial of such an interpretation is to be given little credence. It should be noted that in developing this kind of critique, Freud raises the ad hominem argument to a new importance. It is in *The Future of an Illusion* that Freud makes his position clearest: "Religious ideas have arisen from the same need as have all the other achievements of civilization: from the necessity of defending oneself against the crushing superior force of nature."[3] Therefore, religious beliefs are "illusions, fulfillments of the oldest, strongest and most urgent wishes of mankind . . . . As we already know, the terrifying impression of helplessness in childhood aroused the need for protection—for protection through love—which was provided by the father . . . . Thus the benevolent rule of a divine Providence allays our fear of the dangers of life."[4]

Looking at this argument carefully, we see that in spite of its enthusiastic acceptance by so many, it is very weak. In the first passage, Freud fails to note, his own words notwithstanding, that his arguments against religious belief are equally valid against many of the achievements of civilization, including psychoanalysis itself.

In the second passage Freud makes another strange

claim, namely that the oldest and most urgent wishes of mankind are for the loving protection and guidance of a powerful father. However, if these wishes were as strong as he claims, one would expect the religions that immediately preceded Christianity to have strongly emphasized God as a benevolent father. In general, this was not the case for the pagan religions of the Mediterranean world and is still not the case for such major religions as Buddhism and Hinduism. Indeed, Christianity is in many respects *distinctive* in its emphasis on God as a loving Father. (This emphasis on the father is also characteristic of many of the most primitive religions.)

Let us set aside the preceding weaknesses and turn to another aspect of Freud's projection theory. It can be shown that his theory is not really a part of psychoanalysis—and hence cannot claim support from psychoanalytic theory. To put it differently, Freud's argument is essentially *autonomous*. His critical attitude towards and rejection of religion are rooted in his personal predilections, and his interpretation of religion is a kind of meta-psychoanalysis, or framework, that is not supported by specifically clinical concepts. Indeed, the lack of theoretical connection of the projection theory to psychoanalysis probably accounts for its wide general influence outside the psychoanalytic world. There are two strong pieces of evidence for this interpretation of the projection theory.

First, Freud's theory had been clearly articulated many years earlier by Ludwig Feuerbach in his book *The Essence of Christianity*.[5] Feuerbach's interpretation was well known in European intellectual circles, and Freud, as a youth, read Feuerbach avidly.[6] Illustrative quotations from Feuerbach's work make his influence on Freud clear: "What man misses—

whether this be articulate and therefore conscious, or an *unconscious* need—that is his God"; "Man *projects* his nature into the world outside himself before he finds it in himself"; "To live in *projected dream-images* is the essence of religion. Religion sacrifices reality to the *projected dream*."[7] Throughout the work, Feuerbach describes religion in "Freudian" terms such as "wish-fulfillment" and the like. What Freud did, years later, was to revive Feuerbach's position, articulate it more eloquently, and publish it at a time when the audience for such a theory was much larger. (Between 1841 and 1927, atheistic attitudes had made substantial headway in Western society.) And because Freud is the author, somehow the findings of psychoanalysis are assumed to support the theory. The Feuerbachian character of Freud's position in *Illusion* is also revealed by his use of such key phrases as the "crushing superior force of nature" and the "terrifying impression of helplessness in childhood," which are not psychoanalytic, either in terminology or in meaning.

Second, Freud himself admits that projection theory does not arise from psychoanalytic evidence. In a letter of 1927 to his friend Oskar Pfister (an early psychoanalyst and believing Protestant pastor) Freud wrote: "Let us be quite clear on the point that the views expressed in my book [*The Future of an Illusion*] form no part of analytic theory. They are my personal views."[8]

Nevertheless, Freud implies in *Illusion* that he is very familiar with the psychology of belief in God. Such, however, is not the case. In fact, Freud had very little psychoanalytic experience with patients who believed in God or were genuinely religious.[9] None of his published cases deals with a patient who believed in God at the time of the psychoanalysis. That is, *nowhere did Freud publish a psychoanalysis of the belief in God based on clinical evidence provided by a believing patient.* He never presented publicly any serious psychological evidence for his projection theory or for his other ideas about religion. Instead, Freud's peculiar personal obsession with religion is primarily focused on texts and issues drawn from anthropology, history, and literature—not from any cited psychoanalytic experience. In short, Freud's general projection theory is an interpretation of religion that stands on its own, unsupported by psychoanalytic theory or clinical evidence.

It is important to add that, to the best of my knowledge, there is no systematic empirical evidence to support the thesis of childhood projection being the basis of belief in God. Indeed, the assumption that religious belief is neurotic and psychologically counterproductive has been substantially rejected. Instead, there is now much research showing that a religious life is associated with greater physical health and psychological well-being.[10]

Freud's Unacknowledged Theory of Unbelief

Nevertheless, Freud is quite right to consider that a belief might be an illusion because it derives from powerful wishes or unconscious, childish needs. The irony is that he inadvertently provides a powerful new way to understand an illusion as the psychological basis for rejecting God—that is, a projection theory of atheism.[11]

The central concept in Freud's work, aside from the unconscious, is the well-known Oedipus complex. In the case of male personality development, the essential features of this complex are the following. Roughly at age three, the boy develops a strong sexual desire for his mother. At the same time, he develops an intense hatred and fear of his father and a desire to supplant him—a "craving for power." This hatred is based on the boy's knowledge that his father, with his greater size and strength, stands in the way of his desire. The child's fear of his father may be explicitly a fear of castration by the father, but more typically it has a less specific character. The son does not really kill his father, of course, but patricide is assumed to be a common preoccupation of his unconscious fantasies and dreams. The "resolution" of the complex is supposed to occur through the boy's recognition that he cannot replace his father and through fear of castration which eventually leads the boy to identify with his father—with the aggressor—and to repress the original frightening components of the complex. This resolution is normally completed around age five.

It is important to keep in mind that, according to Freud, the Oedipus complex is never truly resolved, and is capable of activation at later periods—almost always, for example, at puberty. Thus, the powerful ingredients of murderous hate and of incestuous sexual desire within the family are never in fact removed; they are merely covered over and repressed. The adult continues to fear his now-internalized father, who has been incorporated into his super-ego. This fear and self-directed moral hostility are always ready to erupt from the unconscious. Freud explains the neurotic potential of the situation: "the Oedipus complex is the actual nucleus of neuroses. . . . What remains of the complex in the unconscious represents the disposition to the later development of neuroses in the adult."[12] In short, human neuroses derive from this complex. In many cases, this potential is not expressed in any seriously neurotic manner but shows up in critical attitudes towards God and authority, and also in slips of the tongue, transient irrationalities, and the like.

Aside from the personal dimensions of the Oedipus complex, Freud elaborated a cultural-historical model of this complex in *Totem and Taboo*.[13] In this work, Freud proposed an Oedipal and totemic origin of religion. He begins by postulating that the earliest stage of society consisted of "a violent and jealous father who keeps all the females for himself and drives away his sons as they grow up."[14] Freud proposed that such a primal horde, without real culture, was the initial human state. But "one day the brothers who had been driven out came together, killed and devoured their father and so made an end to the patriarchal horde. United, they had the courage to do and succeeded in doing what would have been impossible for them individually."[15] Freud explains the eating of the murdered father by assuming that

> cannibal savages as they were, it goes without saying that they devoured their victim as well as killing him. The violent primal father had doubtless been the feared, envied model of each one of the company of brothers; in the act of devouring him they accomplished their identification with him and each one of them acquired a portion of his strength. The totem meal, which is perhaps mankind's earliest festival, would thus be a repetition and commemoration of this memorable and criminal deed, which was the beginning of so many things—of social organization, of moral restrictions and of religion.[16]

He concludes his argument with a reference to the Oedipus complex:

In order that these latter consequences may seem plausible, leaving their premises on one side, we need only
suppose that the tumultuous mob of brothers were
filled with the same contradictory feelings which we
can see at work in the ambivalent father-complexes of
our children and of our neurotic patients. They hated
their father, who presented such a formidable obstacle
to their craving for power and their sexual desires; but
they loved and admired him too. After they had got
rid of him, had satisfied their hatred and had put into
effect their wish to identify themselves with him, the
affection which had all this time been pushed under
was bound to make itself felt. It did so in the form of
remorse. A sense of guilt made its appearance, which
in this instance coincided with the remorse felt by the
whole group. The dead father became stronger than
the living one had been.[17]

The development of this idea in *Totem and Taboo* closely
parallels Freud's presentation of the Oedipus complex, for
example, in *The Ego and the Id*,[18] but with one interesting
difference. In his discussion of the origin of religion in *Totem*, Freud is more concerned with violence—with the son's
hatred of and rebellion against the father—while in his other
Oedipal writings he places heavier emphasis on the sexual
relationship with the mother.

As a statement about the origins of religion, Freud's interpretation is thoroughly rejected by anthropologists, in part
because there is simply no evidence that culture began with
anything like Freud's "primal horde"—basic family units appear from the very start.[19] Wilhelm Schmidt presents a
simple but devastating critique of Freud's Oedipal totemic
theory about the origin of religion: First, there are many

cultures which have not yet reached a totemic stage; nevertheless, these *pre*-totemic cultures have religion. Second, some rather advanced cultures do not appear to ever have had a totemic stage—yet, like all cultures, they have a religion.[20] No totemic theory—much less an Oedipal one—can account for the origin of religion. Freud's theory of how religion arose is a kind of "just-so story."

Yet in postulating a universal Oedipus complex as the origin of all our neuroses, Freud inadvertently developed a straightforward rationale for understanding the wish-fulfilling origin of the rejection of God. After all, the Oedipus complex is unconscious, it is established in childhood, and above all its dominant motive is hatred of the father (God) and the desire for him not to exist, something represented by the boy's desire to overthrow or kill the father. Freud regularly described God as a psychological equivalent to the father, and so a natural expression of Oedipal motivation would be powerful, unconscious desires for the nonexistence of God. Therefore, in the Freudian framework, atheism is an illusion caused by the Oedipal desire to kill the father (God) and replace him with oneself. To act as though God does not exist reveals a wish to kill Him, much in the same way as in a dream the image of a parent going away or disappearing can represent such a wish. The belief that "God is dead," therefore, is simply an Oedipal wish-fulfillment—the sign of seriously unresolved unconscious motivation.[21]

It is certainly not hard to grasp the Oedipal character of so much contemporary atheism and skepticism. Those whose lives are characterized by promiscuity and atheism are, on Freud's analysis, living out the Oedipal, primal rebellion. And of course the Oedipal dream is not only to kill the father and possess the mother or other women in the group, but also to displace the father. Modern atheism has attempted to accomplish this. Man, not God, is now the consciously specified ultimate source of goodness and power in the universe. Humanistic philosophies glorify him and his "potential" in much the same way religion glorifies the Creator. We have *devolved* from one god to many gods to everyone-a-god. Man, through his narcissism and Oedipal wishes, has seated himself on the throne of God. Thanks to Freud, we may more easily understand the deeply illusory and thoroughly neurotic Oedipal psychology of unbelief.

One interesting example of the Oedipal motivation proposed here is that of Voltaire, a leading skeptic about all things religious who denied the Christian concept of a personal God, of God as a Father. Voltaire was a deist who believed in a cosmic, depersonalized God of unknown character.[22] The psychologically important thing about Voltaire is that he strongly rejected his father—so much so that he repudiated his father's name (Arouet) and took the name "Voltaire." It is not certain where the new name came from.[23] When Voltaire was in his twenties (in 1718), he published a play entitled *Oedipe* (Oedipus), the first of his plays to be publicly performed. The play, which was a major success, recounts the classical legend, with heavy undertones of religious and political rebellion.[24]

Voltaire's rejection of his own father, his rejection of God as Father, and also (in his play) his political rejection of the king—an acknowledged father figure—are all reflections of the same basic need. Psychologically speaking, Voltaire's rebellion against his father and God are directly interpretable as unresolved Oedipal wish-fulfillments derived from childhood. Voltaire's rejection of God is therefore a comforting illusion, and—following Freud's logic—is a belief unworthy of a mature mind.

Diderot, the great encyclopedist and avowed atheist—indeed he is one of the founding brothers of modern atheism—had both Oedipal preoccupation and insight. Freud approvingly cites Diderot's anticipatory observation: "If the little savage were left to himself, preserving all his foolishness and adding to the small sense of a child in the cradle the violent passions of a man of thirty, he would strangle his father and lie with his mother."[25]

A New Theory of Atheism:
The Defective Father Hypothesis

I am well aware that there is good reason to give only limited acceptance to Freud's Oedipal theory. In any case, it is my own view that, although the Oedipus complex is valid for some, the theory is far from a universal explanation of unconscious motivation. There is a need, therefore, for a wider understanding of atheism, especially of the intense kind. Since I know of no theoretical framework other than the Oedipal one, I am forced to sketch something of a new model. But in fact I will develop an undeveloped thesis of Freud himself. In his essay on Leonardo da Vinci, Freud remarks that "psychoanalysis, which has taught us the intimate connection between the father complex and belief in God, has shown us that the personal god is logically nothing but an exalted father, and daily demostrates to us how youthful persons lose their religious belief as soon as the authority of the father breaks down."[26]

This interesting observation requires no assumptions about unconscious sexual desires for the mother, or even about presumed universal competitive hatred focused on the father. Instead, Freud makes the simple and easily understandable claim that once a child or youth is disappointed in or loses respect for his earthly father, belief in a heavenly father becomes impossible. That a child's psychological representation of his father is intimately connected to his understanding of God was assumed by Freud and has been rather well developed by a number of psychologists, especially psychoanalysts.[27] In other words, an atheist's disappointment in and resentment of his own father unconsciously justifies his rejection of God.

There are, of course, many ways a father can lose his authority or seriously disappoint his child: he can be absent through death or abandonment; he can be present but obviously weak, cowardly, and unworthy of respect, even if he is otherwise pleasant or "nice"; or he can be present but physically, sexually, or psychologically abusive. I will call these proposed determinants of atheism, taken together, the "defective father" hypothesis and will seek evidence for it in the lives of prominent atheists, for it was in reading their biographies that this interpretation first occurred to me.

2

Atheists and Their Fathers

SINCE I WILL BE LOOKING at the family life and personal psychology of individual atheists, I will obviously be dependent on biographical evidence. For many important figures of the past biographical data are, unfortunately, scarce. In past centuries, childhood was considered relatively unimportant, and basic facts from this part of people's lives often went unrecorded.

Nevertheless, what I will seek is a pattern found across the lives of many atheists. No single atheist's life is a necessary or sufficient basis for accepting or rejecting the "defective father" hypothesis. The reader should reserve judgment until the biographical evidence has been presented, not only for atheists but also for well-known believers from the same historical periods and societies. If the atheists are understood as an "experimental group," then the believers I will discuss in the next chapter are the "control group." It is *the difference between the patterns* found in these two groups that constitutes the major evidence.

I have selected for study those who are historically famous as atheists. These are great thinkers, typically philosophers, whose rejection of God was central to their
intellectual life and public positions. I will not consider scientists and artists. Normally, scientists have empirical research as their primary concern: their worldview, whether
atheist or theist, is usually not a major preoccupation in their
work. In art—fiction, music, and the visual arts—it is hard
to separate intellectual convictions from works of imagination. Regardless, the people who are treated here are those
who are generally acknowledged as the founders and pro-
moters of modern atheism and unbelief.

But what *is* an atheist? How does this notion relate to
similar positions, such as agnosticism, deism, pantheism, and
the like? I take atheism to mean the rejection of belief in
one God who transcends the world and with whom human
beings may have a personal relationship. In Judeo-Christian
terms, this means a rejection of God the Father.

We begin with what I call the "dead father" syndrome,
for it provides the most clearly identifiable and historically
reliable evidence for the defective father hypothesis. The
dead father is defective for two reasons. First, a dead man
obviously cannot raise children, and in this sense the longer
the father is dead during the course of a child's life the more
defective the father is. Second, the death of a parent is commonly interpreted by young children as a rejection and betrayal. Small children understand death not as a necessity,
but as a choice. The impact of this sense of rejection and
betrayal depends, however, on the nature of the relationship
of father and child. Normally, the death of a father that a
child never knew is less of a rejection than the death of a
father to whom the child was attached.

The impact of a father's death on a child seems to be greatest when it occurs between the ages of three and five. There are at least three psychological reasons for understanding this period as critical. First, there is the psychology of the development of the relationship between a child and his father. In the first year or so, a child is for well-known reasons more attached to his mother. Attachment to his father commonly becomes deeper once the child is able to walk and speak—roughly around the age of two. Of course, a child's relationship with his mother remains strong, but the beginning of a relationship with his father normally occurs about this time, at least in the types of families with which we will be dealing. This relationship then continues to develop in strength. Nevertheless, by the time the child reaches the age of six or seven, the relationship is often diluted somewhat by peer relationships, that is, friendships with schoolmates and other children. In addition, when a child reaches school age, his ability to understand death as something other than a rejection begins to develop. By the time a person is twenty years old, the death of a parent, however painful, is much less likely to be a foundational psychological experience.

A second reason emerges from Oedipal psychology, initiated by Freud and still an important part of contemporary psychoanalysis. In the psychology of boys, the age range three to five is the normal Oedipal period in which the child becomes intensely involved with his father and the mother, as described in the last chapter. Normally, a child resolves the Oedipal conflict by age five through identification with his father. This is a crucial period for the establishment of the child's super-ego (the moral system derived from the father), as well as the formation of his sexual identity. (We are concerned here primarily with male psychology, since the historically important atheists were all men. The atheism of women is a special case and will be addressed later.)

John Bowlby has made an important contribution to the understanding of early personality formation that is very relevant to our discussion: the notion of "separation anxiety." Separation anxiety, the third reason that the early loss of a father is so devastating, is caused by the child's separation from or loss of the loved parent (or parent substitute). Normally, the phenomenon involves the separation of the child from the mother, but a separation from the father can also be a source of this strong and very basic anxiety. Bowlby's work identifies ages two to four as crucial for the establishment of separation anxiety.[1]

DEAD FATHERS

Friedrich Nietzsche (1844-1900)

I will examine atheists and, later, theists, in chronological order by birth. But I begin with Nietzsche because he is probably the world's most famous atheist. In particular, he dramatically rejected Christianity and the Christian God. His best-known pronouncement, "God is dead," is familiar to millions. He was deeply preoccupied with religion all his life and repeatedly and obsessively denounced Christian ideas and those who believed them. In addition, Nietzsche's biographers agree that his thought is profoundly connected to his own peculiar and complex psychology. Nietzsche himself provided the basis for this linkage: "Gradually it has become clear to me what every great philosophy so far has been: namely the personal confession of its author and a kind

of involuntary and unconscious memoir. . . . In the philosopher, conversely, there is nothing whatever that is impersonal; and above all, his morality bears decided and decisive
witness to *who he is*."[2] In a like vein Nietzsche claimed: "I
have absolutely no knowledge of atheism as an outcome of
reasoning, still less as an event; with me it is obvious by instinct."[3] We have, then, good reason to believe Nietzsche's
psychology (unconscious "instinct") bears on his philosophy.

Nietzsche was born in a small village in Prussian Saxony
(Germany) on October 15, 1844, the son of a Lutheran pastor. On both sides of his family there had been numerous
clergymen. One of his biographers notes that although
Nietzsche did not learn to speak until he was two and a half,
"By then he had an extremely close relationship with his
father, who even allowed him in the study while he was working."[4]

Friedrich's father, Pastor Ludwig Nietzsche, died on July
30, 1849, two or three months short of young Nietzsche's
fifth birthday. Pastor Ludwig had been sick for the previous
year from a brain disease. (The postmortem spoke of a "soft-
ening" affecting as much as a quarter of his brain.[5]) Prior to
his death, and even before his illness, he occasionally suffered
from what appear to have been small epileptic seizures that
were of concern to his young wife.[6] Nietzsche often spoke
positively of his father and of his death as a great loss which
he never forgot. As one biographer has put it, Nietzsche
was "passionately attached to his father, and the shock of
losing him was profound."[7] When he was in his early teens,
Nietzsche wrote recollections of his childhood—*Aus meinem
Leben* [From my life]—which included an account of the
day his father died:

When I woke up that morning I heard weeping all round me. My dear mother came in tearfully, wailing "Oh God! My dear Ludwig is dead!" Young and innocent though I still was, I had some idea of what death meant. Transfixed by the idea of being separated for ever from my beloved father, I wept bitterly. The ensuing days were taken up with weeping and with preparations for the funeral. Oh God! I had become an orphan and my mother a widow!—On 2 August my dear father's earthly remains were consigned to the earth. . . . The ceremony began at one o'clock, accompanied by the tolling of the bells. Oh, I shall always have the hollow clangour of those bells in my ears, and I will never forget the gloomy melody of the hymn *Jesu meine Zuversicht* [Jesus my faith].[8]

In this same early autobiography, the young Nietzsche expressed strong religious feeling and identified God with his dead father: "In everything God has led me safely as a father leads his weak little child. . . . Like a child I trust in his grace."[9]

When he was twenty-four, Nietzsche wrote that his father "Died all too soon. I missed the strict and superior guidance of a male intellect."[10] But other comments of Nietzsche's make it clear that although he loved and admired his father, he also saw him as weak and sickly, lacking in the "life force." He wrote in July 1888, six months before the nervous breakdown from which he never recovered, that he is suffering "under the pressure of nervous exhaustion (which is in part hereditary—from my father, who also died from the consequences of a pervasive lack of life force)."[11] Nietzsche made the connection equally clear when he wrote: "My father died at the age of thirty-six; he was delicate, lovable and morbid, like a being destined to pay this world only a passing visit—a gracious reminder of life rather than life itself."[12]

The general weakness and sickness of his father was for Nietzsche also associated, naturally enough, with his father's Christianity. Nietzsche's major criticism of Christianity—of its morality, of the Jesus of Christian theology, and of the whole meaning of the Christian God—was that it suffers from an absence, even a rejection, of "life force." The God that Nietzsche chose was Dionysius—a strong pagan expression of the life force. It is therefore not hard to view Nietzsche's rejection of God and Christianity as a rejection of the weakness of his father. Nietzsche's own philosophy, with its emphasis on the "superman" (or *Übermensch*), on the "will to power," on "becoming hard," on the "blond beast," as well as his well-known denigration of women (He remarked, for example, "You are going to see a woman? Do not forget your whip!" and "The happiness of man is 'I will.' The happiness of woman is 'He will.'"[13]), can all be seen as further expressions of his attempt to identify with a masculine ideal that his father and, by association, his father's religion, were never able to provide.

His search for masculinity was further undermined by the domination of his childhood, after his father's death, by his mother and female relatives: he lived in a very Christian household with his mother, his younger sister, his paternal grandmother and two paternal aunts until he went away to school at age fourteen. It is not surprising, then, that for Nietzsche Christian morality was something for women—a sign of weakness, a slave mentality. In *Ecce Homo*, his autobiography, he stated: "When I look for my profoundest opposite, the incalculable pettiness of the instincts, I always find my mother and my sister—to be related to such *canaille* [rabble, riffraff] would be a blasphemy against my divinity. The treatment I have received from my mother and my sister, up to the present moment, fills me with inexpressible horror: there is an absolutely hellish machine at work here."[14]

At the local school he attended as a young boy, Nietzsche had difficulty relating to other boys. They mocked him as "little pastor" for his serious, self-controlled, pious manners. Because of his myopia, his physically passive temperament, and his frequent illness even as a child, he did not participate in boyhood games. To compensate for his social deficiencies, Nietzsche, even at this young age, emphasized his will—indeed, he had a real desire for self-mastery. He once demonstrated his courage to other children by taking a handful of matches, setting them alight, and holding them in the palm of his hand until a bystander forcibly knocked them to the ground. His hand was badly burned.[15]

Many have noted the strong discrepancy between Nietzsche's harsh, dramatic, and very masculine philosophy—a kind of fantasy persona which he created—and his actual temperament and behavior. "War is another thing," he wrote. "I am by nature warlike. To attack is among my instincts."[16] But in person he was reserved and intellectual, frequently ill with headaches, stomach pains, and other assorted physical problems, including symptoms of syphilis. His health was so bad that he was often bedridden and nursed by his younger sister and his mother.

His philosophy can be interpreted as an intense intellectual struggle to overcome the weakness of his Christian father, a weakness that often seemed to haunt him, as in a dream, which he had as a young boy in 1850, six months after his father died and just before his baby brother died:

I heard the church organ playing as at a funeral. When I looked to see what was going on, a grave opened suddenly, and my father arose out of it in a shroud. He hurries into the church and soon comes back with a small child in his arms. The mound on the grave reopens, he climbs back in, and the gravestone sinks back over the opening. The swelling noise of the organ stops at once, and I wake up. In the morning I tell the dream to my dead mother. Soon after that little Joseph is suddenly taken ill. He goes into convulsions and dies within a few hours.[17]

In short, in Nietzsche we have a strong, intellectually macho reaction against a dead, very Christian father who was loved and admired but perceived as sickly and weak, a representative of what might be called a "death force"—the very opposite of the Superman figure that Nietzsche idealized. As one of his biographers put it, much of Nietzsche's life could be seen as a permanent "quest for the father."[18] Indeed, the Superman may be interpreted as Nietzsche's idealized father figure.

David Hume (1711-1776)

Little is known about the childhood of this important philosopher, who was an early atheist or skeptic at a time when outright atheism was socially and politically dangerous. He came from a relatively prominent and well-to-do family, many of whom were lawyers.[19] David seems to have been on good terms with his mother and also with his slightly older brother and slightly younger sister.[20] A believer as a child, along with his family and most of the society of the time, he was raised as a Scottish Presbyterian. But he lost his faith as a young man, apparently after reading Locke and Clarke.[21] Hume is described as being by temperament amiable and good-natured; many who disliked his ideas found that they liked the man himself.[22] He described his dominant passion as "love of literary fame."[23]

But one fact is the most important: David's father, Joseph, died in 1713 when the philosopher-to-be was only two years old.[24] Hume's biographies mention no relatives or family friends who could have served as father-figures. He was well known as a man without any religious beliefs and for raising many arguments, especially skeptical ones, against religion in any form. Over the course of his career, Hume probably devoted more pages of his writing to the topic of religion than to any other. Therefore, I conclude that Hume was an intense unbeliever and that he fits the "dead father" hypothesis.

Bertrand Russell (1872–1970)

Bertrand Russell is generally understood to be the most prominent English atheist, and his position, primarily focused on the rejection of Christianity, is well known. It is perhaps best summarized in his collection of essays *Why I Am Not a Christian* (1957), but it was clearly expressed many decades earlier when many of his essays were first published.

Both of Bertrand's aristocratic parents lived on the margin of radical politics.[25] Lord Amberly, Russell's father, whose childhood diaries are filled with religious concerns, became a freethinker in adulthood. He died when Bertrand was four years old. Young Bertrand was present at the end, and there is a description of him at his father's deathbed. To make matters worse, Russell's mother had died two years earlier. Bertrand was subsequently cared for by his grandparents, Lord John Russell and Lady Russell, but his grandfather, a rather distant figure, died in 1878 when Bertrand was six. Hence, his only functional parent was Lady Russell, who was known as the "Deadly Nightshade."[26] This woman, Bertrand's greatest childhood influence, was by birth a Scottish Presbyterian, by temperament a puritan. The atmosphere of her religion was "a mournful Christian humility."[27]

Religion at Pembroke Lodge, his grandmother's residence, was a rather eclectic Protestantism and was the foundation and structure of everyday life.[28] Although Bertrand had an interest in religion all his life, he very early became an agnostic or atheist. The religion that he rejected was clearly that of his grandmother. Russell's daughter Katherine described it as "the only form of Christianity my father knew well, the life of this world was no more than a gloomy testing ground for future bliss. . . . My father threw this morbid belief out the window."[29] Russell mocked Christians, according to his daughter, "for imagining that man is important in the vast scheme of the universe . . . yet [he] thought man and his preservation the most important thing in the world."[30] "I believe myself," she concluded, "that his whole life was a search for God, or, for those who prefer less personal terms, for absolute certainty."[31]

Russell's only other parent figures were a string of nannies to whom he often grew very attached: when one of his beloved nannies left, eleven-year-old Bertrand was "inconsolable."[32] He soon discovered that "one way out of the sadness of these constantly changing companions was reading, retreating into a distant and increasingly abstract world."[33] The early deaths of his parents and grandfather, plus his frequent "lost" nannies, could easily be the source of his incredible desire for certainty: "I wanted certainty in the kind of way in which people want religious faith."[34] In addition, while Bertrand was growing up, he was very much a loner who had no really close friend.

Marked by his early years of lost loves and solitary living at home with tutors, Russell described himself as follows: "My most profound feelings have remained always solitary and have found in human things no companionship. . . . The sea, the stars, the night wind in waste places, mean more to me than even the human beings I love best, and I am conscious that human affection is to me at bottom an attempt to escape from the vain search for God."[35]

Although this passionate, lonely man sought certainty and clarity with monomaniacal fervor, he remained a man of contradictions: "Do we have free will? He said 'no' writing philosophy; but acted 'yes' and wrote 'yes' when his moral passions were engaged. Is there progress in the world? He might say 'no' and make fun of the sillier versions of it, but he acted 'yes' and based his life of hope on it."[36]

Jean-Paul Sartre (1905-1980)

Sartre has been one of the most famous atheists of the twentieth century. His existential philosophy is based on atheism, and his position is well summarized in his own words: "If one discards God the father, there has to be someone to invent values. . . . To say that we invent values means nothing else but this: life has no meaning a priori. Before you come alive, life is nothing; it's up to you to give it a meaning, and value is nothing else but the meaning you choose."[37]

Sartre's father, Jean-Baptiste, died in 1906 when young Jean-Paul was only fifteen months old.[38] Ronald Hayman, a biographical historian, has studied Sartre's relationship with his mother, grandfather, and stepfather quite thoroughly. After the death of his father, Sartre and his mother lived with his maternal grandparents. His grandfather, Charles Schweitzer, was young Jean-Paul's tutor, but the relationship was never emotionally close. Instead, Sartre cultivated a very intimate relationship with his mother. As Hayman observes, "[Sartre's mother] concentrated her emotional energy on her small son, who had everything done for him: he was washed, dressed, undressed; his shoes were put on, his hair brushed. . . . He was fair, rosy-complexioned, with plump cheeks and curls; endless photographs were taken."[39]

This idyllic and "successful" Oedipal involvement came to a painful close with the remarriage of his mother when Sartre was twelve. He was not close to his new stepfather—indeed, he strongly rejected him. When his mother remarried, "Sartre sustained a loss from which he never fully recovered. He had felt completely secure in his possession of her; as he had grown closer [to her] in adolescence, the only rival male, his grandfather, had been growing weaker and less threatening."[40] Sartre, therefore, grew up without a father, without paternity in any real psychological sense. Put differently, Sartre's real father died (abandoned him) very early, his grandfather was cool and distant, and his stepfather took Jean-Paul's beloved mother away from him.

Young Sartre stayed with his grandparents while his mother moved into an apartment with her new husband. Although the stepfather, Joseph Mancy, made an effort "to win the affection of his stepson," he found it impossible.[41] It was only a year or so after his mother's remarriage that the adolescent Sartre concluded to himself: "You know what? God doesn't exist."[42]

Some fifty years later in *Les Mots*, his autobiography, Sartre treats the death his father as a piece of good fortune: Sartre did not even have to forget him.[43] Nevertheless, Jean-Paul was obsessed with fatherhood all his life—and obviously he never got over his fatherlesness. Some of this is clearly detected by Hayman, who quotes from a Sartre screenplay: "I wanted to kill my father in you."[44] Meanwhile, in true Oedipal fashion, Sartre surrounded himself with a long line of loving younger women.

A great deal of evidence for Sartre's continued paternal preoccupation comes from a recent biography by Robert Harvey, appropriately titled *Search for a Father: Sartre, Paternity and the Question of Ethics.*[45] We can only touch here on some aspects of Sartre's obsessional preoccupation with paternity, his father, and God. He repeatedly condemned and ruminated about fatherhood. His philosophy was about the "self-made man" and about man becoming God. He often wrote about fathers as metaphors for weight, as burdens who crush their sons. In contrast, lightness (even unbearable lightness) was the consequence of being fatherless. A typical condemnation of paternity is found in *Les Mots*: "There is no good father, that's the rule. Don't lay blame on men but on the bond of paternity which is rotten. To *make* children: nothing better; to have them: what iniquity! Had my own father lived, he would have lain on me full length and crushed me. As luck would have it, he died young."[46] Yet in Sartre's lifelong critical treatment of paternity, there is so much ambivalence that it is obvious that "he doth protest too much."

How does Sartre know a father would have been a heavy burden?: He never really experienced his father. Harvey says of Sartre's play *The Flies* that "underlying Sartre's wild en-

thusiasms for unfettered freedom lies nostalgia for responsibility as *embodied* in the missing father."[47] This claim is
backed up by Harvey's observation that Sartre's writings,
"with predictable regularity," set up "a relationship between
the absence of moral responsibility . . . and an absent father
or the lack of paternal sentiment in a potential father."[48]

Almost everywhere Sartre "paints fathers in hideous col-
ors,"[49] though there are a few exceptions. Again, one won-
ders where Sartre got the psychological and experiential basis
for his judgments. Certainly not from his own father's presence. We must conclude, instead, that his father's absence
was such a painful reality that Jean-Paul spent a lifetime
trying to deny the loss and to build a philosophy in which
the absence of a father and of God is the very starting place
for the "good" or "authentic" life.

Albert Camus (1913-1960)

Albert Camus, another French atheist and existentialist, also
fits the pattern. His father, Lucien, died in 1914 at the Battle
of the Marne, when Albert was one year old.[50] Camus reveals the importance of this loss in his autobiographical novel
The First Man (1995), published thirty-five years after the
writer's death.[51] His father is a central preoccupation of this
work.

Part one, "Search for the Father," recounts the visit of
the protagonist (named Jacques, representing Camus) to his
father's grave in France, which he had never visited; chapter
five is completely about his father. A passage in which Camus
describes an important teacher and father figure is particularly telling: "This man [his teacher] had never known his
[Jacques's] father, but he often spoke to Jacques of him in a

rather mythological way, and in any case at a critical time he knew how to take the father's role. That is why Jacques had never forgotten him."[52] In short, a melancholy search for his father runs through this last and strongly autobiographical work—a sadness broken by Jacques's commitment to life, love, and a kind of solidarity with all people.

Arthur Schopenhauer (1788-1860): *A Father's Suicide*

Arthur Schopenhauer, known as the great pessimist, had a somewhat positive relationship with his father, Floris, before his father's death in 1805, apparently the result of suicide: the elder Schopenhauer jumped (or fell) out of a third-story window into a canal.[53] Floris was a wealthy and cosmopolitan merchant, something of a free thinker, who was an admirer of Voltaire. Although during his childhood Arthur was very often away at school or separated from his father when the latter was traveling, the father-son relationship was reasonably strong and positive. A recent biographer, W. P. Bridgwater, writes that the father's death was "the darkest day of his [Arthur's] life."[54]

Schopenhauer's relationship with his mother, on the other hand, was very negative. Even in his infancy and childhood, his mother's love was apparently absent or meager. Rudiger Safranski, another major biographer, identifies Schopenhauer as one who did not "receive primary love, maternal love."[55] His mother, who had not "intended" to have Arthur, saw her child as the cause of a painful loss of personal freedom, a symbol of "her own renunciation."[56] He grew to detest her, and they were estranged for most of their lives. After some short periods of happiness in his late childhood, Schopenhauer knew no such period again. He never married; he broke from his sister and apparently never had any other emotionally sustaining relationships.

Young Arthur's recollections of his early years "speak almost exclusively of loneliness and fear." He was looked after principally by a nursemaid and servants: "as a child of six, my parents, returning from a walk one evening, found me in deep despair because suddenly I thought I had been abandoned by them forever." Arthur's father began to take a serious interest in his child when the boy was about eight—roughly the beginning of Schopenhauer's short period of positive memories.[57]

Though Schopenhauer's mother pronounced his father's death accidental, Arthur himself "blamed his mother for his father's suicide."[58] Floris's death occurred when Arthur was seventeen, and the connection of this event to Schopenhauer's rejection of God is implied in his retrospective observation that "As a young man, I was always very melancholic, and on one occasion, I was perhaps eighteen years old then, I reflected even at early age: This world is supposed to have been made by a God? No, much rather by a devil."[59]

Arthur had one serious conflict with his father. His father insisted on the boy's becoming a merchant, and until his father's death Arthur obeyed this paternal injunction, if reluctantly. The father's suicide, however, released the son from this necessity and ultimately permitted Schopenhauer's philosophical career to develop.

He suffered from a great sense of loneliness—a loneliness rooted in childhood fear of abandonment. To him, all was vanity, all was empty and meaningless—hence perhaps his affinity for a Buddhist type of atheism, where the emphasis is on emptiness, on nothingness. His philosophy rejected metaphysical reasoning about religion and the transcendent; he also rejected the Enlightenment emphasis on a progressively positive future for mankind. He strongly focused on suffering and on the human will as central to understanding life.

ABUSIVE AND WEAK FATHERS

Thomas Hobbes (1588-1679)

This great philosopher and political theorist is sometimes called the father of modern analytical philosophy, and his harsh, absolutist social philosophy remains widely influential. He is certainly one of the great founders of modern thought.

Hobbes's father, also Thomas, was the vicar of a small Anglican church outside London. There was little to admire about him. He is described as ignorant, of a choleric temper, and given to cardplaying; apparently, he sometimes fell asleep during the services over which he presided. When another parson provoked him at the church door, there was a fight in which the elder Hobbes struck his opponent, after which he fled beyond London. His family never saw or heard from him again, and he died in obscurity. A childless uncle who was a successful tradesman took over the financial responsibility for the family. The uncle's wealth enabled the young Hobbes to attend good secondary schools and then Oxford. There is no comment, however, by Hobbes or his biographers on any affection for this uncle.[60] He appears to have been a rather distant figure.

In his published works, Hobbes's handling of religion was typically skeptical, though he leaves unclear his own personal position on subjects such as the existence and nature of God. His public position is perhaps best summarized by R. S. Peters:

> [Hobbes's] technique was always to push radical probing to the limit, and when the basis for the traditional doctrines seemed about to be cut away, the sovereign [the king] was summoned as a sort of *deus ex machina* to put everything in its orthodox place. . . . It is difficult to say whether his suggestions that the sovereign should pronounce on such matters as the creation of the world and the attributes of God was a subtle piece of irony, a pious protestation to protect himself against the charge of atheism, or yet a manifestation of his overwhelming conviction that there must be nothing touching the peace of the realm that the sovereign should not decide.[61]

During his lifetime Hobbes was frequently believed to be some kind of atheist or skeptic—though he never clearly publicly said so. Of course, if he had declared his skeptical or heretical views openly, his life would have been in immediate danger. A recent Hobbes scholar, A. P. Martinich, has said of Hobbes that he was "either an atheist or deist, and that in either case he was intent on subverting belief in revealed religion."[62] This is not an especially surprising conclusion, given that Hobbes's philosophical system was rationalist, materialist, and Epicurean.[63] All scholars agree that he was consistently and intensely anticlerical. (It is easy to see the seeds of this in his father's behavior.) It can be fairly said that Hobbes was a major historical enemy of the personal God of Christianity.

Jean Meslier (1664-1729)

The case of Jean Meslier is in some respects an ambiguous one, since we have little information about his childhood and youth. But since his case is also extraordinary, and because he was an important figure, especially for Voltaire, he turns out to be well worth our attention.

Meslier has been described as "perhaps the least restrained free-thinker of the French Enlightenment" and "one of the most notorious examples of apostasy."[64] He was a parish priest who lived in complete obscurity and whose radical views only became known after his death when his one work, his *Testament*, was published to considerable scandal. The work is intensely anti-Christian, specifically anti-Catholic, and is a general attack on the *ancien régime* as well. It is atheistic, antiauthoritarian, even anarchistic, and indeed communistic—revolutionary in every respect. The intensity of his violent feelings is remarkable: "In the *Testament* there flows such a torrent of bitterness, aversion, anger, hatred and revolt that, even after two hundred years, as Paul Hazard put it, 'one cannot read it without shuddering.'"[65]

Unfortunately, we know very little about Meslier's father and childhood. But we do know that he became a priest, not from any sense of calling to the religious life, but because his father insisted.[66] In other words, his life as a priest—a life which was a very long lie—was forced upon him by his father. It is also clear that he was moderately wealthy from family money, and it is likely, though of course not certain, that his father's continued financial support was contingent on Meslier's becoming a priest.

Meslier's life as a priest appears to have been fairly respectable. He was charitable to the poor and spoke in favor of orphans and the oppressed. On the other hand, the political historian Igor Shafarevich notes in *The Socialist Phenomenon* that on the cover of his *Testament* Meslier wrote: "I came to know the errors and the misdeeds, the vanity and the stupidity of the people. I hated and despised them." After describing the peasants' suffering, Meslier remarked: "It is justly said of them that there is nothing more corrupt, more crude and deserving of contempt."[67]

Of the few details known about his life two are quite interesting: First, Meslier was repeatedly ordered by his bishop to cease having servant girls—typically described as his "cousins"—living with him, as the situation was a cause of scandal.[68] Second, at one point he came into violent conflict with the local nobility—more precisely, the local *seigneur*—and with his bishop over what he considered a matter of social justice.[69] Indeed, he approached open rebellion in his conflict with the bishop. While one may applaud aspects of Meslier's social conscience, one cannot fail to note that the lord and the bishop are father figures.

There is not enough information to make an obvious case for Meslier's having had an abusive father—though any father who would force a son who felt no call to the priesthood to become a priest and a celibate could justifiably be called abusive. In any case, for Meslier to have lived a life of such complete hypocrisy—for he maintains that he was *never* a believer[70]—would very likely have caused him intense internal conflict. He must have struggled constantly with his own sense of honesty, on the one hand, and fear and shame, on the other. Whatever his internal motivations may have been, they certainly cannot be considered "rational." In other words, the motivation for his violent atheism was psychological, not philosophical.

Meslier is important for his influence on others, such as Voltaire (who edited the first printed version of Meslier's work), Diderot, and d'Alembert.[71] Meslier is also important because in him we see more clearly than in any figure of the Enlightenment the true spirit of violence that found expression in the French Revolution's "Reign of Terror."

Voltaire (1694-1778)

As noted earlier, Voltaire is not a true atheist, but rather a deist who believed in an impersonal God.[72] Yet he is famous as a powerful critic of religion, especially Christianty, with its understanding of a personal God. Much of Voltaire's criticism was aimed at the social and political influence of the Church, as well as at various popular theological attitudes. I have selected him because of his enormous historical importance, because so much of his critical writing dealt with religious issues, and because his criticism of religion was so frequent, intense, and radical.

Voltaire's real name was François-Marie Arouet. The Arouet family was comfortably well off, the father a successful businessman—a gift that Voltaire demonstrated in his own life. Voltaire's mother died in her son's seventh year. When he was ten, Voltaire was sent away to a Jesuit school where he was an accomplished student and a poet.[73] He made friends both with his Jesuit teachers and his fellow students, and he retained many fond memories of his seven years at the school and of particular Jesuit teachers.

François-Marie Arouet changed his last name to Voltaire as a young man—a choice surely indicative of his negative attitude toward his family and his father in particular. A recent biographer, A. D. Aldridge, has noted that Voltaire demonstrated neither affection for his parents nor attachment to family traditions: "Although Voltaire wrote extensively about his father, he said virtually nothing in his favor."[74] As a young man in his twenties, Voltaire is known to have signed his name "de Voltaire"—which suggests a socially ambitious nature and his feeling of superiority toward his his father.[75]

There appear to have been several reasons why Voltaire distanced himself from his father. A recently discovered letter of Voltaire's makes it clear that he believed himself to be the illegitimate son of a certain Rochebrune, a lyric poet and family friend. As Aldridge points out, Voltaire's belief "does not mean that he was illegitimate, merely that he preferred to be considered another man's bastard rather than his legal father's son."[76] In any case, his belief that his legal father was not his biological father is hardly a sign of filial devotion toward Monsieur Arouet.

Another cause of Voltaire's rejection of his father was their quarrels. At one time, his father was so angry with his son for his interest in the world of letters (rather than law) that he authorized having his son sent to prison or into exile in the West Indies.[77] The only member of his family with whom Voltaire had amicable relations was an older sister, Marguerite-Catherine.[78] This sister later had children, and one of them, under her married name of Madame Denis, became well known as Voltaire's niece and housekeeper. Aldridge noted that "Two centuries later it has been discovered that she was also his mistress."[79] Voltaire had a number of mistresses and never married.

Jean d'Alembert (1717-1783)

This great French rationalist and *philosophe* was in many re-spects the co-editor of the *Encyclopedia* with Diderot.[80] D'Alembert, besides being an outstanding mathematician, also wrote important philosophical works. A skeptical deist who ended up a materialist and atheist, he took an active part both in defending the *Encyclopedia* against its religious and monarchist critics and in the radical intellectual life of the time.[81] He was well known as an enemy of religion in general and all denominations in particular, especially the Catholic Church, and most especially the Jesuits. At the time of his death he was described by an opponent as a "vio-lent and hardened unbeliever."[82]

He was sensitive and witty, a popular animator of dis-cussions at various salons, and was greatly respected for his integrity. He maintained friendships with orthodox reli-gious intellectuals as long as they were not fanatics. His major weakness, according to friends and foes alike, was a certain timidity, and at times cowardice, in response to en-emies or confrontation.

D'Alembert's childhood was unusual and clearly sub-stantiates the defective father hypothesis. Jean was the ille-gitimate son of the celebrated salon hostess Madame de Tencin and an artillery officer, Louis-Camus Destouches. At his birth, his mother abandoned him in a wicker basket at the baptistery of Notre Dame de Paris, a little church called Saint Jean le Rond (the round church of Saint John), and that is the name that was given to the baby, Jean le Rond. He was soon taken to a foundling home and then sent out to be nursed for six weeks. When his father, who had been away in America at the time of his son's birth, returned, he had the child's upbringing entrusted to a glasscutter's wife, a certain Madame Rousseau. Except for one visit to Jean as a boy—a visit arranged by his father—there was apparently never any contact between d'Alembert and his natural mother, and d'Alembert always thought of Madame Rousseau as his real mother. His father helped finance d'Alembert's education, but a few facts should be emphasized. D'Alembert was never officially recognized by Destouches as his son, though the boy presumably knew who his father was.

Destouches died in 1726 when Jean was only twelve, around the time he was sent to school. Enrolled under the last name of Daremberg for reasons which remain obscure, Jean himself changed it to "d'Alembert," using the noble "d," suggesting a desire for family status. The school he attended was largely Jansenist (a puritanical form of Catholicism). He was an outstanding student, though he showed a marked aversion to theology. Next he studied law, and then medicine, but he eventually became a largely self-taught mathematician and philosopher. During all this time he continued to live in a cramped room at the home of his foster mother, Madame Rousseau. Indeed, he stayed there until he was forty-seven years old, never marrying. When he finally moved, it was only because of bad health.

In short, as a boy d'Alembert did not know a father's love or even have an official father, or an official last name, and his own name had no particular meaning for him. After his father's death, the Destouches family did, however, support Jean and follow his career with interest.

Baron d'Holbach (1723-1789)

This *philosophe* has been called "the foremost exponent of atheistic materialism and the most intransigent polemicist against religion in the Enlightenment"[83] He was no doubt one of those dozen or two "known unbelievers" prior to the French Revolution referred to by James Turner.

D'Holbach was born Paul Henri Thiry to a family of modest landowners in the German Palatinate.[84] We know nothing about the character of his father, Johann Jakob Thiry, or his mother Katerina, née Holbach. However, when Paul Henri was a young child he was sent to live with his maternal uncle, François-Adam Holbach, who had recently amassed a great fortune. Subsequently this uncle bought for himself noble lands and titles—hence the aristocratic *d'*Holbach, "of" Holbach.[85] As a boy or young man, Paul Henri acquired from his uncle his name, his title, and his wealth. The boy's early life was spent at his uncle's home in Paris and then on his uncle's estate in Hesse. In 1744, when he was twenty-one, he entered the University of Leyden under the name Paulus van Holbach.[86] In 1749 he returned to Paris and became a French citizen. Later, in Paris, he bought a position that made him French nobility.[87] He is described as a man who "apparently sought at times to inflate his origins."[88] He bought a house in Paris on the Rue Royale that for the next twenty-five years was a prominent center for free-thinkers. Here, the immensely wealthy d'Holbach hosted on a regular basis what is known as his "coterie"—his circle—many of whose members were the major minds of the French Enlightenment. Diderot, for example, was a regular member.[89]

Paul never appears to have spent much time with his

father or mother. He took his uncle's name, but he is not on record as ever having made any positive comments about him. He also, as noted, later showed a desire to inflate his "origins." In any case, he was permanently separated from his father whose name he rejected and whose social status he found inadequate.

Ludwig Feuerbach (1804-1872)

This German philosopher, who first formulated the projection theory, caused a tremendous stir with the publication of his *Essence of Christianity*. Another famous critic of religion, Ernest Renan, wrote in the 1850s that Feuerbach would have been called the Anti-Christ if the world had ended then.[90]

Ludwig was born into a distinguished and gifted German family. His father, Anselm, was a prominent jurist and criminologist (who still ranks very high in the history of legal and criminological thinkers). Anselm was a liberal Protestant Kantian of progressive social views, but was difficult and undiplomatic. His relationships with colleagues were frequently very stormy. Eugene Kamenka describes Anselm as "fiery and impulsive," a man who was known in the family as "Vesuvius."[91]

The dramatic event of young Ludwig's life must have been his father's affair with Nannette Brunner, the wife of one of his father's friends.[92] Nannette and Anselm lived openly together in another town, and she bore a child whom they named Anselm. This affair began in 1813 when young Ludwig was nine years old and lasted until Nannette's death in 1822, when Anselm returned to live with his wife—Ludwig's mother—Wilhelmine.

In summary, Feuerbach's prominent father publicly rejected his family and lived with and had a child by another woman. Eventually, his father, known as "Vesuvius," returned to live with his legal family—but only because his mistress had died. This was in the early 1800s when such a relationship must have caused great scandal.

Samuel Butler (1835-1902)[93]

Samuel Butler, an Englishman, had a father and grandfather who were clergymen. It was expected by his family that he would enter the ministry in his turn; but when he graduated from Cambridge in 1858, he refused to enter the church on the grounds of religious doubt. He then spent several years in New Zealand; on his return to England in 1864, he devoted himself to painting, music, and writing. Between 1877 and 1890 he produced a series of works of scientific controversy.

Butler occupies a sort of middle case in this study because in addition to scientific works, he published various works of fiction, including a satire (*Erewhon*, 1872). He worked on his most famous book, *The Way of All Flesh*, from 1873 to 1885, but this work was not published until the year after his death in 1903.

Butler was tyrannized in his youth by a pious and unfeeling father who beat him. Like the character in his posthumous novel, he revolted against the beating and piety of his father, as well as his family and Victorian mores generally. He considered that his father never liked him; he, in return, could recall no time when he did not fear and dislike his father. They were rivals, and in this rivalry sought every opportunity to belittle or criticize the other. The brutal treat-

ment by his father came to color his view of people generally. In his biography of Butler, Malcolm Muggeridge notes
that "there is hate in every reference Butler makes to his
childhood. His family, it seemed to him, were banded together in a conspiracy to make him unhappy, to hurt and
deform him, to deprive him of those things for which his
soul longed. Hatred accumulated all through his childhood,
and for the rest of his life he had to carry it about with him,
a great load of hate weighing him down." Butler had, in
short, "built a world around his father, hated the world he
had built, then, horrified, realized that he lived in it, and
must go on living in it to the end of his life."[94]

The popularity which came to Butler after his death
(dinners attended by ever greater numbers of well-known
writers were held in London every year to commemorate
his writings) has been said by one commentator to

centre in Ernest's [the Samuel Butler character in his
often autobiographical novel] revolt against the pro-
prieties of the Victorian Age. Ernest quickly became
a symbol of the tame culture hero impatient with the
customs of his age; in our time he remains a paradigm
of youth revolting from adults, of son shedding the
straight jacket imposed by father. More particularly,
Butler ridicules the prevailing concept of family and
child-rearing, the theory of public-school education,
the reigning religious and moral shibboleths, and the
sacred values by which the English middle classes lived.
. . . While Butler's nihilism is ever present, generating
corrosive criticism of Victorianism, he substitutes nothing very attractive. For the traditional marital and
child-rearing codes he offers parenthood without marriage or filial responsibility. For the ethics he aban-

dons he proposes smug hedonism—an Epicurean con-
templative life of lukewarm pleasures and minimized
pains.[95]

The misunderstanding and bitterness between father and
son grew, with the son seeing himself as a defenseless youth
bravely standing up to parental brutality, and the father seeing himself as the sacrificing father bitterly disappointed in
a beloved son.

Butler stopped saying his prayers and, in Muggeridge's
words, came "to see that words were like darts with poi-
soned tips that he could plunge into the breasts of his en-
emies . . . and bring his father's church, his father's God, his
father's hopes and beliefs and standards of behavior tum-
bling down one after the other. With words he was formidable."[96]

His life-long hatred of his father, complicated by his
desire not to offend his father so greatly as to jeopardize his
inheritance (shades of Meslier?), led to a situation in which
he remained in the church—but without being part of it—
and lived and wrote against it. He was "a Broad Churchman, but without a church, so that what he said in effect was
that he remained broad. To be a Broad Churchman is bad
enough, but to be broad without being a churchman is ter-
rible; and this is what Butler was—an earnest atheist."[97]

His fame in the early part of the twentieth century rested
on his rejection of Victorian morality. Butler was homo-
sexual and lived a hedonistic adult life. Again, in Muggeridge's words, large numbers of people

were yearning to be relieved of the burden of family
relationships, which, since their religious sanction had

gone, had become irksome. They wanted someone to tell them that, not only was it not wrong to detest their mothers and fathers and sisters and brothers (not yet wife; that a later harvest), but right and proper, advanced, fashionable; they wanted to feel that, far from being undutiful, they were victims of an oppressive and cruel system, which only their particular virtue had enabled them to survive. *The Way of All Flesh* made them feel this. . . . Butler's self-pity became universalized, and a generation fed on it.[98]

Sigmund Freud (1856-1939)

That Sigmund Freud's father, Jacob, was a disappointment or worse to his son is generally agreed upon by his biographers. Jacob Freud was a weak man, unable to provide for his family. Instead, the money seems to have come from his wife's family and others.[99] Furthermore, Freud's father was passive in response to anti-Semitism. Freud recounts a frequently-noted episode told him by his father, in which Jacob allowed an anti-Semite to call him a "dirty Jew" and knock his hat off.[100] Young Sigmund, on hearing the story, was mortified at his father's failure to respond strongly, at his father's weakness. Sigmund Freud was a complex and in many respects an ambiguous man, but all agree that he was a courageous fighter and that he greatly admired courage in others. As a young man, Sigmund several times physically stood up against anti-Semitism, and of course he was one of the greatest of intellectual fighters.

Jacob's defectiveness as a father, however, probably went deeper than incompetence and weakness. Specifically, in two of his letters as an adult, Freud writes that his father was a sexual pervert and that Jacob's own children suffered as a result.[101] Finally, it should be recalled that in proposing the Oedipus complex, Freud placed hatred of the father at the center of his psychology. It is not unreasonable to assume that this expressed, at the least, his strong unconscious hostility to and rejection of his own father.

The connection of Jacob to God and religion was also present for his son. Jacob was involved in a kind of reform Judaism when Freud was a child; the two of them spent hours reading the Bible together, and later Jacob became increasingly involved in reading the Talmud and in discussing Jewish scripture.[102] In short, for Sigmund this weak, rather passive "nice guy" was clearly connected to Judaism and God, and also to a serious lack of courage and to sexual perversion and other weaknesses very painful to young Sigmund. It is not surprising then that we owe to Freud the autobiographical insight, "Psychoanalysis . . . daily demonstrates to us how youthful persons lose their religious belief as soon as the authority of the father breaks down."[103]

H.G. Wells (1866-1946)[104]

The English writer and "social philosopher" H. G. Wells had an immense influence on popular culture in the early decades of the twentieth century. His public debates—with, among others, Hilaire Belloc—and the vast sales of his *Outline of History* (over two million copies) made him "one of the great popularizers and one of the most influential voices of his age."[105] His books led some to adopt atheism and others to write against it.[106]

Born to working-class parents in London, Wells was the fourth child of a gardener and his wife. Within six months of his parent's marriage, his father had lost his job and, with the help of a loan, purchased a china shop. The father knew nothing about business and, in any event, was not a hard worker. Rather than earn a living at some other kind of work, he made a little money playing professional cricket. He spent increasingly long periods at the local cricket grounds and in pubs, where he gambled. The more time he spent at cricket, the less time he had for his wife and family—and for his shop. The neglect and rejection of his wife took its toll on the marriage, which became increasingly unloving and cold. Sarah, Wells's mother, was the virtual manager of the shop and home, while her husband, Joseph, shirked his responsibilities and was frequently away. Wells's biographer Michael Coren writes that "a sense of mutual hostility, bordering on contempt, was exacerbated by fear of conceiving more children. . . . The couple began to sleep in separate rooms. Sarah became bitter and sullen, Joseph became detached, apathetic, and began to contemplate leaving the country or selling the shop in order to make a new life elsewhere for himself."[107]

Two years before Wells was born, his older sister, Frances, aged nine, died suddenly of appendicitis. His mother suffered an almost total emotional collapse and developed a monomaniacal obsession with her dead daughter. She blamed herself, then her husband, and though she pleaded with Joseph for support, "he seemed unable to provide anything more than a perfunctory shoulder."

Distant from his father and brothers, Wells in his autobiography does not hide his contempt for his father or his anger at the condition to which Joseph had reduced his mother. Wells draws a clear connection between the collapse of his mother's pietistic faith and his own hatred of

God. In a revealing passage, he comments on his father's lack of compassion for his grieving mother:

> Joe [his father] was apt to say, "There, there, Saddie," and go off to his cricket; . . . my mother had to do all her weeping alone. It is my conviction that deep down in my mother's heart something was broken when my sister died two years and more before I was born. Her simple faith was cracked then and its reality spilled away. I got only the forms and phrases of it. I do not think she ever admitted to herself, ever realized consciously, that there was no consolation under heaven for the outrage Fate had done her. . . . She wanted me to believe in order to stanch that dark undertow of doubt. In the early days with my sister she had been able so to saturate her teaching with confidence in the Divine Protection, that she had created a prodigy of Early Piety. My heart she never touched because the virtue had gone out of her. . . . I was indeed a product of Early Impiety.[108]

He comments poignantly on his mother's prayers that God "make Joe better," but adds bitterly: "It was like writing to an absconding debtor for all the answer she got." Whether it is Joe the father or God the Father who gave no answer seems to make no difference to Wells, because for him both were equally absent. He soon came to hate God intensely and concludes this portion of his life story by noting that

> Religion and love, except for her instinctive pride in her boys, had receded imperceptibly from her life and left her dreaming. Once she had dreamt of reciprocated love and a sedulously attentive God, but there was indeed no more reassurance for her except in

dreamland. My father was away at cricket, and I think she realized more and more acutely as the years dragged on without material alleviation, that Our Father and Our Lord, on whom to begin with she had perhaps counted unduly, were also away—playing perhaps at their own sort of cricket in some remote quarter of the starry universe.[109]

The few letters from Wells to his father exhibit a cursory sort of cordiality. His account of his father's death contains no sadness, no expression of loss and provides simply the basis on which Wells can comment that his forebears tended to die quickly and without much suffering.

MINOR ATHEISTS

John Toland (1670-1722)

Toland was an early deist and singularly controversial figure who caused much alarm in orthodox Christian circles in England and Ireland. Robert E. Sullivan, an important biographer of this curious man, describes Toland's God as having "no ultimate causal nature and as without any providential relationship to human affairs. Furthermore, Toland left no prayers, meditations or anecdotes suggesting he believed in a personal God."[110]

Toland was born in a remote Irish parish; he is said to have been the bastard child of a Roman Catholic priest. Sullivan writes with regard to this issue: "The vehemence of his denials, and the studied vagueness of his efforts to produce a pedigree are at any rate suggestive. In attempting to obscure his origins he even tampered with his given name."[111]

Toland was raised a Catholic. At the age of fourteen he

converted to Protestantism. Local sources report that he was anticlerical even at this young age, and, although he changed religion a number of times in his life, his anticlericalism always remained with him.

In his early youth he was a shepherd. By his nineteenth year he was a rootless and lonely, but bright young man, hoping for success and driven by inner turmoil. Apparently there is no record of his family, and in his many letters he never refers to any family member.

Educated in Scotland, he began to write on religious subjects, at first supporting Calvinist rigor against the more "liberal" Arminianism. He went to Holland for further schooling, supported by churchmen on whose side he was writing at the time. His subsequent religious writings and behavior, and his several switches in allegiance, meant that he had no permanent denominational or other support.

In Leiden, his vanity and strong desire for celebrity are said to have gained him a negative reputation. His standing was not helped by his habit of frequenting coffee houses and taverns, in one of which he is reported to have burned a copy of *The Book of Common Prayer*. He spent much of his time speaking against the Scriptures, railing against priests, and the like. In 1695 he published his major and most controversial work, *Christianity Not Mysterious*. This "freethinking" critique of Christianity was instantly recognized as heretical and put Toland in considerable jeopardy. Unfortunately for Toland, even his influential friends such as John Locke soon distanced themselves from him because of his vanity and a tendency to over-familiarity.

Toland continued his checkered career, spending time on the European continent, eventually returning to England. In his later years, he apparently maintained his religiously heterodox beliefs but wrote primarily on topical political issues. He was always in difficult financial straits and never found either an adequate income or permanent intellectual support.

Richard Carlile (1790-1843)

Carlile, an Englishman, became an ardent advocate of deistic and then atheistic and other radical ideas. He was an active journalist, publishing his and other writers' works; in the early 1800s, he organized some of the first groups to publish skeptical views on religion. He was also one of the first to publicly advocate birth control. His importance in the history of free thought and atheism—along with Robert Taylor—is attested by his inclusion in Herrick's *Against the Faith: Essays on Deists, Skeptics and Atheists*, a book that covers many of the major figures in the atheist-agnostic tradition.[112]

What is known about Carlile's childhood is that "his father was a cobbler, exciseman, schoolmaster, and soldier and apparently published essays on mathematics. He was given to drink, perhaps the reason for his son's strong advocacy of sobriety, and died when Richard was four. His mother and elder sisters sustained the family."[113]

Carlile was apprenticed in the tin-plate trade, but rebelled against his hard master; thus he showed at an early age his defiant temperament. At this time—in his twenties—he had no special interest in religion or politics. But after 1815 he began to write radical letters to the press and from then on he became an increasingly visible and controversial public figure known for his attacks on religion.

Robert Taylor (1784-1844)

Taylor was another English freethinker. He was born into a
fairly well-to-do family, but his father died when he was six
or seven years old.[114] At the age of fourteen, he was sent by
his uncle to apprentice to Samuel Partridge, the house surgeon at General Hospital near Birmingham. Partridge—
apparently something of a father-figure—admonished Taylor
never to give his mind to religion. But, though Taylor did
complete his medical training in London, he did convert,
rather briefly, to Anglicanism. At the age of twenty-five, he
went to Oxford and, upon his graduation in 1813, was ordained a deacon. At the time, "he was highly thought of
and set for an Anglican career, aided by personal charm and
obvious scholarship."[115] After about four years, his views
began to change, and he came to the conclusion that Christianity in particular, and all religions in general, were a great
curse to humanity. His incredulity soon resulted in his becoming persona non grata in the church, and in 1824 he
formed a society to question Christianity. In 1829, he joined
with Carlile and "set off on an infidel mission across the country to meet their supporters and debate believers."[116]

Along with Carlile, he became a public advocate for the
radical rejection of Christianity. In 1833, he married a rich
widow, left public life, and settled in France, working as a
surgeon until his death.

CONTEMPORARY ATHEISTS

Madalyn Murray O'Hair (1919-?)

One of America's best-known atheists, Madalyn Murray

O'Hair was responsible for bringing the lawsuit that led the United States Supreme Court, in the 1960s, to ban prayer in the public schools. Until her disappearance, she remained active as an atheist. Her son's memoirs, which open when he is eight years old, reveal the tone of his family life: "We rarely did anything together as a family. The hatred between my grandfather and mother barred such wholesome scenes."[117] He claims that he did not know why his mother hated her father so much—but hate him she did. In the opening chapter of the book, he reports a very ugly fight in which O'Hair attempted to kill her father with a ten-inch butcher knife. She failed but screamed, "I'll see you dead. I'll get you yet. I'll walk on your grave!"[118]

Whatever the cause of O'Hair's intense hatred of her father, it is clear from her son's book that it was deep, and that it went back into her childhood; abuse—psychological and possibly physical—is a likely cause.[119]

Albert Ellis (1913-)

Another contemporary atheist worth considering is the American clinical psychologist Albert Ellis, who is renowned for his Rational Emotive Therapy (RET), which he has developed over several decades at his Manhattan-based institute. Ellis is highly critical of religion as being intrinsically irrational. He frequently voices his criticism of religious belief and practice in very harsh and crude, even vulgar, language. I have personally heard his criticisms on two occasions and was informed that his intense and insulting language on those occasions is typical.

Some years ago, at a conference in Dallas, Ellis and I spoke one after the other. Ellis spoke as an atheist psychologist, and I as a theistic psychologist. Each talk lasted about forty minutes, and since we both sat on the dais, we heard each other's papers. Ellis heard a short form of the thesis of this book. After the session was over, he told me as we walked out together that the thesis did not apply to him since he had a good relationship with his father. I replied that a psychological hypothesis is fortunate to be valid in even 50 to 60 percent of the cases.

Back in New York City, I sent a copy of my talk to a friend who is a book editor, Dr. George Zimmar, who was at that time working for the Praeger Publishing Company. A few weeks later, he phoned to tell me that he had read the paper and, incidentally, that it was helpful for understanding Albert Ellis. I was quite taken aback and told Zimmar that Ellis had personally denied the relevance of my thesis to his life. "Well," my friend replied, "we are publishing his biography, and I was reading the page proofs last night; I think he fits your hypothesis." Later, when the biography appeared, I read about Ellis's childhood. The author, Daniel Wiener, describes Ellis as suffering from "parental neglect and serious illness throughout his childhood."[120]

Ellis was born into a Jewish family in 1913. His mother "spent a minimum of time and concern on her sons, daughter and husband."[121] When he was age five, Albert had a serious illness for which he was hospitalized. "His family seldom visited him for most of the year he was in the institution."[122] Albert's brother, Paul, was his closest and life-long friend. Their father was often absent and, by their teens, he had abandoned the family. Manny, Albert's only good friend (aside from his brother), never did meet the father.[123] His mother seldom cooked, was often in bed, and bustled about as a kind of opinionated chatterbox: "Her sons treated her with almost total disrespect."[124] The mother remained ineffectual and rather distant. When the economic depression hit the country in the 1930s, the two brothers had to support themselves and their mother.

Young Albert is described as a brainy, skinny, cool, and unemotional child. But a boy who has been abandoned by his father and has had to support himself and his mother must have been deeply wounded by the situation. Albert and his brother managed their financial situation well and eventually attended college—no thanks to their father. His achievements took courage, psychological toughness, and a denial of those emotions created by a father's neglect and abandonment.

LOOKING BACK at our thirteen major historical rejectors of a personal God, we find a weak, dead, or abusive father in every case. Two prominent recent examples—O'Hair and Ellis—also provide support for this pattern. By way of comparison, we now turn to look at the childhoods of well-known believers from the same historical periods.

3

Theists and Their Fathers

I T IS OF COURSE POSSIBLE that the evidence of defective fathering in the lives of atheists is simply a reflection of the social conditions of the time. What is required, then, is a comparison of the atheists with a control group of theists. If the fathers of prominent believers over the past three hundred years were no different from those of unbelievers, then the findings of the previous chapter do not constitute evidence for the defective father hypothesis. In order to explore this important issue, I will examine the early years of historically representative theists, after which we can more adequately evaluate the biographical evidence from the lives of atheists.

I have selected these theists not just for their piety or general prominence during their lifetime, but because each is known for his intellectual defense of Christianity or Judaism. Each was a part of the religious counter-response to the atheistic or skeptical intellectual attitude typical of the modern period.

Blaise Pascal (1623-1662)

Pascal is well known both as a great mathematician and as a great religious writer. He lived at a time and in a place (Paris) of considerable general skepticism about religion, yet wrote *Les pensées* (*Thoughts*), a powerful and imaginative defense of Christianity and an attack on skepticism.

Pascal's father, Etienne, who was a wealthy judge, was also an able mathematician, knowledgeable about science, and well versed in Latin and Greek. He was also known as a good man and a good Catholic. Pascal's mother died when he was three years old, and Etienne Pascal took over the education of young Blaise and his older and younger sisters, giving up the law except for the management of his financial affairs and the continuation of his interest in mathematics. Entirely "home-schooled," young Blaise was clearly a child prodigy both in science and mathematics. Jean Steinmann, one of the major biographers of Pascal, gives something of the flavor of the household and of Blaise's early genius: "At mealtimes they discussed the explosion of gunpowder, the way water rises in pumps, the effects of lightning, the refraction of light, and the reason why certain objects float on the surface of water. Blaise experimented with sound by tapping with his spoon on a pewter plate, then on a copper jug and on a silver plate. He discovered that sound is produced by vibrations, and as soon as he had learnt to write, attempted a short treatise on acoustics."[1] Later, when he was twelve years old, he discovered many of the elements of geometry on his own, in spite of his father's reluctance to teach that branch of mathematics to one so young.

In 1651, when Blaise was twenty-eight years old, Etienne Pascal died in Paris in the presence of Blaise and Blaise's sister, Jacqueline. On the death of his father, Blaise wrote a short treatise, "The Death of a Christian," in the form of a letter to his other sister and his brother-in-law. From this letter emanates peace and confidence in the salvation of his father.

Pascal is an extremely complex and challenging figure. Nevertheless, he certainly fits the hypothesis and is a fine example of a boy whose father loved him and who returned that love. After his father's death, Blaise powerfully presented the theistic position during one of the first periods when it had become unfashionable to do so—especially in the scientific and philosophical circles in which he moved.

George Berkeley (1685-1753)[2]

Born in Ireland, this famous philosopher is known for his analysis of perception—a theoretical approach that is subjectivist in character—which was a major critique of materialism and its atheistic implications. He became, at age forty-nine, a bishop in the Church of England in Ireland. He was a strong believer who, for example, tried to found a college in colonial America (Bermuda) to convert the natives and counter the growth of irreligion in American society. We know that George had a younger sister, and he appears to have been the eldest of six brothers.[3] William Berkeley, his father, was a man of position and fairly well-to-do, a former officer who fought under the Earl of Galway. George's mother "was an aunt to General Wolfe, father of the famous general of that name."[4]

The Berkeleys brought up their six sons as gentlemen, sending them to good schools—three to the university. Both parents died in the same week when each was nearly ninety years old.[5] The philosopher was close to his brothers and had an amiable personality. As one biographer puts it, "Berkeley held his head high and showed no trace of undue family pride; he was of gentle birth; his folks were well connected but not ennobled."[6]

George and his wife, née Anne Forster, had four children who survived infancy—Henry, George, William, and Julia—in whose education, it is reported, George found his chief happiness. He referred to his children with great affection. He described Julia "as such a daughter," as of "starlight beauty," and "so bright a gem."[7] The death of his son William was a serious blow to him.

Throughout his life, the philosopher and bishop gave generously to the poor and often wrote about how to improve local social conditions. As a mature man, in his mid-thirties, he was described by Atterbury, an important contemporary, as of "so much understanding, so much knowledge, so much innocence, and so much humility, I did not think had been the fashion of any but angels, till I saw this gentleman." Alexander Pope said of him that he was a man with "every virtue under heaven."[8] On July 14, 1753, he died as he lay on a couch, while his wife read to him from the Letter to the Corinthians.[9]

Looking over his life as a whole, we certainly know that George's father was alive for much of the philosopher's life, and there is no evidence of any estrangement or bitterness between them. We also know that Bishop Berkeley was a serious believer who publicly represented and defended his faith throughout his adult life.

Joseph Butler (1692-1752)[10]

Joseph was the youngest of eight children of a well-to-do cloth merchant. His father had retired to live in a house called the Priory. Joseph first went to a Latin school, then to another academy, before going to college. He decided to enter the Church of England though his father preferred that he become a Presbyterian. He was ordained an Anglican priest at twenty-six and much later became Bishop of Durham. Butler is most famous for his *Analogy of Religion, Natural and Revealed, to the Constitution and Course of Nature* (1736).

During his early years, he sometimes received money from an elder brother. He never married, but remained in contact with his siblings and their children throughout his life. At his death, he left most of his estate to his nephews and nieces. By temperament, he was calm, and his intellectual position strongly supported reason over the emotional aspects of religion. But he was also described as easily persuaded to give money to beggars.

We know little about his relationship to his father, except that his father was still alive when he went off to Oxford in 1715, when he was twenty-three. We also know that Butler's father was persuaded, after a little trouble, to accept Butler's choice of the Church of England. There is no evidence of estrangement, and one can presume an adequate father-son relationship in the case of this Christian thinker and clergyman.

Thomas Reid (1710-1796)[11]

This famous philosopher was a believer and a long-time

Protestant minister who was primarily known for his contributions to philosophy. He wrote in a simple, clear, impartial, earnest style. His philosophy represented a lucid and strong common-sense position—very much a response to Hume's skepticism. Reid's most important work was *An Inquiry into the Human Mind on the Principles of Common Sense*, published in 1764.

Thomas's father, the Reverend Lewis Reid, was also a minister, and Thomas lived at his father's manse until he was about twenty-three years old.[12] His father died in 1762, when Thomas was fifty-two years old and, as noted, he followed in his father's footsteps professionally. All these details are signs that the father-son relationship was positive. Lewis Reid was respected for his "piety, prudence, and benevolence, inheriting from his ancestors simplicity of manners, and literary tastes."[13]

Young Thomas, who had an elder brother and two sisters, was educated at home until his tenth year, then spent two years at a local parish school. At twelve, he went to Aberdeen to enter Marischal College where he first encountered the intellectual currents of the time—especially the views of George Berkeley. Graduating in 1726, he continued studies in theology and was eventually ordained as a Presbyterian minister—a profession at which he was a success because of what is described as his mild and beneficent activity. The seriousness of his religious life is revealed by his theological vocation, by his theistic philosophy, and by his personal life, and is documented by a long and very moving prayer found among his papers after his death. It was written when he was thirty-six years old and was occasioned by his wife's grave illness. It reads, in part,

O God, I desire humbly to supplicate Thy Divine
Majesty in behalf of my distressed wife, who is . . .
in imminent danger of death, if Thou, . . . do not
in mercy interpose Thy almighty arm, and bring her
back from the gate of death. I deserve justly, O Lord,
that Thou shouldst deprive me of the greatest com-
fort of my life, because I have not been so thankful
to Thee as I ought for giving me such a kind and
affectionate wife. I have forgot Thy goodness in
bringing us happily together by an unforeseen and
undesigned train of events, and blessing us with so
much love and harmony of affection. . . . O Lord,
accept my humble and penitent confession of these
my offences, which I desire to acknowledge with
shame and sorrow, and am resolved by thy grace to
amend. . . . Lord, pardon if there is anything in this
presumptuous, or unbecoming a humble penitent
sinner; and, Lord, accept of what is sincerely designed
as a new bond upon my soul to my duty, through
Jesus Christ, my Lord and Saviour.[14]

Mrs. Reid recovered, and their successful marriage
lasted some fifty years, producing five children who survived infancy.[15] Reid is said to have been "amiable" to
his family and to have delighted in young children.[16] He
was regarded as a steady friend who was charitable to
others.

Edmund Burke (1729-1797)[17]

Born in Dublin to a Protestant father and a Roman Catholic mother, Edmund was the second son of Richard Burke,
an attorney of some prominence. (He was named for the
poet Edmund Spenser, a distant relative of his mother.)

According to the custom at the time, Edmund was raised in his father's religion, the Anglican Church of Ireland,[18] but because of his mother's religion he had Catholic sympathies and a great belief in religious tolerance.

Because of Edmund's delicate health his mother took him from Dublin as a very young boy, with his older and younger brothers, to live with her father in a village in southern Ireland (County Cork), where he spent five years of his boyhood. He was very close to his mother, and also to his maternal uncles James, Patrick, and Garret. Edmund always remembered his three uncles with great affection—particularly Garret, whom he described as "one of the very best men, I believe, that ever lived, of the clearest integrity, the most genuine principles of religion and virtue, the most cordial good-nature and benevolence that I ever knew or, I think, ever shall know . . . for of all the men I have seen in any situation I really think he is the person I should wish myself, or anyone I dearly loved, the utmost to resemble."[19]

Besides his uncle Garret, another father-figure for Edmund in this small Irish town was the schoolmaster, O'Halloran. Burke liked him very much and many years afterwards visited him to pay his respects. In addition, when Burke was around twelve, he became a serious admirer of another schoolmaster at Ballitore School, a Quaker by the name of Abraham Shackleton. His admiration for Shackleton and his lifelong friendship with Shackleton's son Richard confirmed Burke's commitment to religious tolerance.

As for his own father, the relationship seems to have been one of some respect but also of emotional distance, not only because he spent many years away from his father, but because his father was clearly a difficult person, described as having "an irritable temperament."[20] Edmund is known to have had some disagreements with him as a young man; in particular, Edmund's decision to reject a legal career led to his father's angry withdrawal of his allowance. Nevertheless, he admired his father: "My father left me nothing in the world but good principles, good examples; which I have not departed from." "The fact is, that my father never did practice [law] in the country, but always in the superior courts: that he was for many years not only in the first rank, but the very first man of his profession in point of practice and credit."[21]

Edmund entered Trinity College, Dublin, in 1743 and completed his studies in 1748. He also studied law for a while in London. His father spent a good deal of money on his son' s education, and despite Edmund's words— "My father left me nothing in this world"—he inherited considerable property from his father. Burke married, and it was a happy marriage; he and his wife had two sons, both of whom died in childhood.

Edmund Burke became a great British statesman and intellectual, who is important for his political theory. He championed conservatism—indeed, he is often considered the founder of modern conservative political thought. His writings are in direct opposition to the radical Jacobinism expressed in the French Revolution, the most important of which is *Reflections on the Revolution in France* (1790). Burke was very much opposed to abstract philosophical schemes and ideologies. He argued strongly for the validity and wisdom of tradition. Though he advocated religious tolerance, he was a great champion of the importance of religion as a central component of tradition and major barrier to unbridled rationalist schemes. One of his major criticisms of the French Revolution, of which he had a real horror, was its hostility to religion: "We are not the converts of Rousseau; we are not the disciples of Voltaire; Helvetius has made no progress amongst us. Atheists are not our preachers."[22] Likewise, "We know, and it is our pride to know, that man is by his constitution a religious animal; that atheism is against not only our reason, but our instincts; and that it cannot prevail long."[23]

For Burke, God and religion were a positive and necessary foundation for the state, indeed for all civilized political life.[24]

Moses Mendelssohn (1729-1786)[25]

The great Jewish philosopher, Bible translator, exegete, and literary scholar Moses Mendelssohn was the son of a poor Torah scribe named Menachem Mendel Dessau. Moses himself took the surname "Mendelssohn"—"son of Mendel"—when as an adult he began to consider himself part of a larger German culture.

Moses was at first carefully educated at home by his father, then by other Jewish scholars.[26] He was so highly motivated and so intellectually gifted that at age fourteen he left his hometown of Dessau to study with Rabbi David Frankel in Berlin. Rabbi Frankel was probably his major teacher, but he had several other outstanding Jewish teachers who, along with Moses's father, provided intellectual role models. In Berlin, Moses also studied the thought of German philosophers such as Gottfried von Leibniz and Christian von Wolff and that of the English philosopher John Locke.

In 1750 Moses became the tutor to the children of a silk manufacturer in Berlin named Issak Bernhard, who in 1754 took Moses into his business. By this time, Moses already had a high reputation for wisdom and was called by some the "German Socrates." Gotthold Ephraim Lessing, whom Mendelssohn met in 1754, modeled the hero of his play *Nathan the Wise* on Mendelssohn.

Mendelssohn earned his living as a merchant; his philosophical and intellectual life were carried out in what leisure time he had. In 1762 he married a plain, poor young woman named Fromet Guggenheim; they had three sons and three daughters, each of whom is worthy of a brief entry in the *Jewish Encyclopedia.* One of his grandsons, Felix Mendelssohn, became a well-known composer and musician.

Moses Mendelssohn was a major force in the emancipation of Jews from punitive German laws and in their assimilation into German cultural life. He was also a staunch intellectual defender of the existence of God and of the immortality of the soul. His most important book is probably *Phaedo, or on the Immortality of the Soul* (1767), in which he spoke out against the materialist philosophy of the day.

His personal relationships with his father and his teachers and his relation to his religious faith showed no signs of hostility or rejection—as his very choice of the name "Mendelssohn" certainly indicates. Although Mendelssohn promoted the assimilation of Jews into German cultural and political life, it was never at the expense of their Jewish faith. Mendelssohn's own religious and philosophical life was centered around his belief in God.

William Paley (1743-1805)[27]

This major English theologian and moral philosopher is famous for his *Natural Theology* (1802), as well as many other writings. His father, a vicar and minor canon in the Church of England and the owner of a small estate, died at the age of eighty-eight, when William was well over fifty. Paley's mother died in 1796 when he was fifty-three.[28] William followed his father as a clergyman in the Church of England.

Paley was at first educated at his father's school, then in Aberdeen. In October 1759, Paley rode on horseback with his father to begin his studies at Cambridge. His father predicted that his son—his oldest child—would be a great man "for he has by far the clearest mind I ever met with."[29]

Paley—tall and eventually stout—was married, had nine children, and is reported to have been a sociable and affectionate father and husband. He outlived all his children except for one daughter, Mrs. Carmichael, who cared for him in his old age.[30]

William Wilberforce (1759-1833)

This great evangelical Christian and English parliamentarian devoted most of his life to abolishing the English slave trade, a task at which he largely succeeded. He was born into the well-off Wilberforce family, long established in Yorkshire. He was the only son of Robert Wilberforce, a partner in a very successful business. Young William was a small, frail child with weak eyesight. When grown, he reached only five feet three inches, but his lively and sociable spirit and his energy were appreciated by all. At seven, he went to a local grammar school.

William's father died when he was nine years old, and a year later his mother sent him to live with a childless paternal uncle and aunt. It was a warm and congenial household in which William experienced the religious piety of early Methodism. His biographers agree that this experience laid the groundwork for his later conversion.

It was in this religious household that he met John Newton, the author of the famous hymn "Amazing Grace." Newton was a former slave-trader whose life was transformed by his conversion. It would have been at the impressionable age of ten or eleven, in this "enthusiastic" Christian home, that young Wilberforce first heard of the "problem" of slavery. William was enthralled by Newton's sermons and stories, "even reverencing him as a parent when [he] was a child."[31]

His mother, a Protestant of the more subdued and traditional type, was unenthusiastic about religious enthusiasm—for example, early Methodism—and removed William from the home of his aunt and uncle where he had been so especially happy. Much later, William said, "I deeply felt the parting. I loved them as parents; indeed I was almost broken-hearted at the separation.'"[32]

He returned to Yorkshire and became part of the active society that surrounded him and his family there. At seventeen he went to Cambridge where he was, as he put it, generally idle, but nevertheless did moderately well at his studies. He was such a positive personality—he was especially gifted at singing—that he was popular despite his small stature and lack of athletic prowess.

Shortly after finishing at Cambridge, he sat for election to Parliament, and to his delight he won. At the age of twenty-one he represented one of the largest counties in England. Through his close friendship with the young Pitt and his own considerable talent, he became a successful political figure. In his mid-twenties he had a conversion, precipitated by various friendships and by books he was reading. He became an evangelical Christian devoted to ending the slave trade. He was soon a major voice for abolitionism.

François René de Chateaubriand (1768-1848)

The great French romantic writer Chateaubriand is famous for his romantic novels, but was nonetheless a defender of Christianity. In 1802, shortly after the French Revolution, he published *The Genius of Christianity*. This book, which was extremely popular at the time, defended Christianity by appealing to the emotions, to aesthetic judgments, and by drawing on the power of associations. Thus the book fits within his generally romantic, rather than rationalistic, approach.

Chateaubriand was the youngest of ten children, of whom six survived childhood. His father came from an old aristocratic family that had become impoverished, but he was able to reestablish the family fortune in the shipping industry through his energy and abilities; he started as a lowly sailor and eventually became a sea captain, and then a ship owner.

Chateaubriand's father was cut from very different cloth than Pascal's father: he was a rather cold, distant, and temperamental man, and appears to have been more interested in his eldest son and heir than in François, the last of his children. Nevertheless, he was lively, strong, energetic, and admirable, and François was never estranged from his father or rejected him. He died in 1786, when François was eighteen. Many years later, Chateaubriand said of his father, "I have treated our most praiseworthy of fathers as he deserves. I have depicted him as he was, a man of courage and genius."[33]

Friedrich Schleiermacher (1768-1834)

Friedrich's father, Gottlieb Schleiermacher, was a Reformed pastor and a chaplain in the Prussian army (a Reformed Church is Protestant in the Calvinist, rather than the Lutheran, tradition).[34] His father, in his younger days, had identified with rationalist and Enlightenment theology, but through contact with Moravian Protestants he had experienced a devotional renewal. He and his wife were determined to give their children a Moravian upbringing, and in 1783 Friedrich, with his sister and brother, joined the Moravian boarding school at Niesky. Schleiermacher's biographer Keith Clements notes that "Friedrich was never to see his parents again. His mother died a few weeks after his entry to the school, and his father's journeys with the regiment prevented any further contact beyond their frequent correpondence." The result was that the community of the Brethren became Friedrich's new family home "in his formative and adolescent years." He did spend his first fifteen years with his natural parents. At seventeen, Friedrich transferred to the Moravian theological seminary at Barby. "The warm-hearted devotion to Jesus, with the shared life of rigorous study, vital worship and close personal relationships gave him his primary religious experience and its influence never left him, even though he was to leave the Moravians."[35]

When he began to have serious doubts about Moravian teaching in his late teens, Friedrich wrote to his father to explain them. The result was a serious theological conflict between father and son: Gottlieb was deeply disturbed at his son's position, which smacked of Enlightenment thought. But their relationship survived the disagreement, and by 1790, when Schleiermacher was twenty-two, the father and son had clearly been reconciled for some time.[36]

Schleiermacher became famous as a theologian who emphasized the importance of religious experience as central to the Christian life. His widely influential theology was a major reponse to the rationalism of the Enlightenment and is best known as presented in his famous *On Religion: Speeches to its Cultured Despisers* (1799). Other important works include *Outline of a Critique of Previous Ethical Theory* (1803) and *The Christian Faith* (1821-2).

John Henry Newman (1801-1890)[37]

This great English religious figure was a convert from Anglicanism to Catholicism and, years later, a cardinal in the Catholic Church. A central figure in the Oxford Movement of the 1840s, he made major theological contributions to the discussion of Anglican-Catholic differences. More important, perhaps, he developed both a clear and critical understanding of modernism and a rational response to modernism, for example, in *An Essay in Aid of a Grammar of Assent* (1870). He is also known for his *Idea of a University* (1852, 1859) and for his autobiographical work *Apologia Pro Vita Sua* (1864).

Newman was the eldest child of John and Jemima Newman. His father was a banker; the family was a happy one, and young Newman had younger brothers and a sister with whom he generally got along well. In 1808, at age seven, he went to private boarding school where he was studious and strong-willed.

In March 1816, when Newman was fifteen, his father went bankrupt. All debts were paid, but it was a tragedy; his father then headed a brewery, but family circumstances remained straitened. Interestingly enough, it was shortly after this event, in August 1816, that John Henry fell ill and experienced a conversion. The experience was not a violent or a highly emotional conversion; instead, it seems to have been brought on by the reading of religious books which made a deep impression on him.

In December of 1816, Newman traveled with his father and a curate friend of theirs to Oxford University. He began his studies at Oxford in June 1817; he was an outstanding student. While he was at Oxford his father came to collect his son for at least one Easter vacation and heard young John Henry praised for his academic accomplishments. At Oxford, he worked long hard hours and remained in steady contact with his parents through letters. In 1821, when Newman was twenty years old, he wrote to his mother that they ought to be thankful that they were so happy and united a family.[38] In 1822, Newman was elected a fellow of Oriel College—a great surprise and honor. Two years later, when Newman was twenty-three, his father died.

As his father was dying, Newman hurried home, and was there in time to be with him as he expired. Newman wrote about their final encounter: "He knew me, tried to put out his hand, and said 'God bless you.' He died three days later."[39]

Alexis de Tocqueville (1805-1859)

The selection of Alexis de Tocqueville as an example of a theist may be somewhat surprising. After all, Tocqueville is renowned for his political, sociological, and cultural analysis and commentary. Certainly his best-known work, especially in the United States, is *Democracy in America* (1835, 1840). He was never directly engaged in the philosophical and theological debate over theism. Nevertheless, he was an outspoken advocate of religion, not only as an important part of a nation's life, but as a fundamental and necessary part. His position was really quite unusual for the time, when the atheistic and skeptical interpretations of culture and society were becoming standard in Europe. I cited a passage from Tocqueville in the introduction, in which he expresses his awareness of and admiration for religion as foundational in American social and political life. But in many respects, Toqueville's underlying intellectual position in all of his writings was theistic in character. In a letter written in 1836 to a boyhood friend, he expresses his theistic understanding of the political process:

You seem to me to have understood the general ideas
on which my programme rests. What most and
always amazes me about my country [France], more
especially these last few years, is to see ranged on
the one side men who value morality, religion and
order, and upon the other those who love liberty and
the equality of men before the law. This strikes me
as the most extraordinary and deplorable spectacle
ever offered to the eyes of man; for all the things
thus separated are, I am certain, indissolubly united
in the sight of God. They are all holy things, if I
may so express myself, because the greatness and the
happiness of man in this world can only result from
their union. It seems to me, therefore, that one of
the finest enterprises of our time would be to dem-
onstrate that these things are not incompatible; that,
on the contrary, they are bound up together in such
a fashion that each of them is weakened by separation from the rest. Such is my basic idea.[40]

Alexis was the youngest of three sons born to parents of the high French aristocracy. The Tocquevilles were
a family known for their "deeply rooted Catholic Christianity" and "aristocratic pride and dignity."[41] His parents' marriage and lives were permanently scarred by the
French Revolution; they were almost executed during the
Terror, and many of their relatives and friends were put
to death. Young Alexis spent his early childhood near
Paris with his family and was educated to a large extent
by Abbé Lesueur, who had also been in charge of his
father's education a generation before. The "abbot" (he
was not an abbot in the strict sense of the word, but rather
a priest) had been chosen by Alexis's grandmother—a

deeply pious Catholic. Thus, he was both a father and a grandfather figure for young Alexis. While he was in America, in 1831, Alexis learned of his tutor's death. He was deeply moved and wrote to his brother Edward: "I loved our good old friend as I did our father. . . . Never again shall we meet a man whose whole faculties and affections are centered upon ourselves. He seems to have lived for us alone."[42] These quotations show us that Alexis loved the Abbé and that he loved his father.

The religious life of Alexis de Tocqueville was apparently that of a devout Catholic as a child and youth. During his early adulthood he turned to a general Christian theism. In the last years of his life (he died in his mid-fifties), he returned to his Catholic faith. In any case, he never became an atheist or skeptic, and in his public intellectual life he was always supportive of religion.

Samuel Wilberforce (1805-1873)

Samuel—later Bishop—Wilberforce was a very prominent nineteenth-century English believer. He is well-known as one of the major debaters in the conflict in the 1860s over Darwinian evolutionary theory. His father, discussed earlier, was also a public figure—indeed, a kind of national institution. In spite of the time-consuming activities of his public life, the elder Wilberforce was a most devoted and dutiful father. Of his four sons, three became clergymen and "were notably devout."[43]

To young Samuel, the third son, his father often wrote long letters; over six hundred of them are extant.[44] "This fond father sat down at his table and, line after line, page

after page, poured out admonition, exhortation, information, and above all, love—all in the most unreserved manner."[45]   On one occasion, when Samuel was twelve years
old and had recently gone away to school, his father wrote,
"I hope my dear Lamb will, during his absence from his
earthly father and mother, look up the more earnestly to
that heavenly Father who watches over all that put their
trust in Him, and has given special encouragement to
children to apply to Him for every needful blessing."[46]
And in another letter he says, "Oh my dear, dear Boy, how
earnestly I wish and hope that God may bless you with
his Holy Spirit. I shall pray for you tomorrow between
2 and 3 o'clock, and again between 8 and 9."[47]

When Samuel was preparing to go off to Oxford, his
father arranged to spend many weeks with him before his
departure. Samuel described this convivial time spent
together at the seashore, at Barmouth, in notebooks that
still survive.

Throughout his life, Samuel remained devoted to his
father and to his father's memory. He and his brother
Robert edited and published a six-volume biography of
their father, as well as two volumes of his letters.[48]

Sören Kierkegaard (1813-1855)

This great Danish religious thinker is regarded by many
as the founder of existentialist philosophy. His major works
are *Fear and Trembling* (1843), *Philosophical Fragments* and
The Concept of Dread (1844), and *Either/Or* (1845). His more
explicitly Christian works are *Sickness Unto Death* (1849),
and *Training in Christianity* (1850).

Since Kierkegaard was one of the first great students of psychology of the modern period—indeed of any period—he is of special interest. His story provides a remarkable instance to support our thesis.

He was born in Copenhagen, the seventh and last child of an elderly father and his younger wife. Sören's father was a prosperous businessman and left enough money to Sören so that he never needed to work. His father was, as Kierkegaard's biographer Melville Chaning-Pearce has put it, "a passionate, austere, guilt-haunted and, in a puritan form, deeply religious man" who "dominated both by attraction and repulsion the life of his son."[49] Sören himself was a somewhat sickly child, hypersensitive and very intellectual, who accepted his father's imposed austere faith. Nevertheless, "as he grew to manhood he fluctuated between a reverent affection for and resentment and rebellion against his father. But the latter's influence remained dominant to the end and was the mould of his piety. It was from his father that he learned how to live with God: 'I have, quite literally, lived with God as one lives with one's father.'"[50]

Sören, at the age of seventeen, left high school and went to the university in Copenhagen, planning to be ordained in the Lutheran church. For several years, he lived the life of a brilliant, but self-indulgent and wild, undergraduate. He threw himself into the intellectual life of the university and gained a reputation for his polemics and wit. This phase of his life ended when he was twenty-two years old, in 1835. He experienced a major loss of faith—what he called "a great earthquake." At this time his hostility toward his father came to a head, precipitated in part by his father's confession to him of having had sexual relations with his wife, Sören's mother, a cousin and household domestic, before they were married.

The immediate and primary effect of this psychological quake was to drive Sören to defy not only his father but also God. He became violent and bitter in his rejection of his father and of things religious, abandoning religion for philosophy. His life of dissipation increased. Nevertheless, he "recognized later, rebellion against his father implied rebellion against God"[51]: "It is so difficult to believe because it is so difficult to obey."[52] His rebellion peaked in 1836, but by his twenty-fifth birthday, in May 1838, he was reconciled with his father, by then an old man of eighty-two. At the time, his father took the "opportunity, it seems, to make a full confession of both his failings and his faith to his son. Three months later, his father died, and Kierkegaard evidently believed that, by overtaxing his strength by so costly a confession, he had sacrificed himself for his son's sake. The reconciliation was complete; the broken link between father and son was reforged more firmly than before, and the obedience and gratitude which Kierkegaard had latterly denied to his father alive, he rendered doubly to him dead."[53]

In his reconciliation, Kierkegaard displayed the psychological insight for which he is so famous: "It was the full significance of fatherhood which his reconciliation had discovered, of the Divine Fatherhood as of the human fatherhood which is the moral type of that 'great tradition.' It is in the light of this flash of comprehension that he can say that Christian truth is true 'because my father told me so.'"[54]

Baron Friedrich von Hügel (1852-1925)

Friedrich von Hügel, born in Florence of an Austrian father and Scottish mother, chose to live in England and wrote his works in English. His father, Baron Karl, had fought in the Napoleonic wars, but in 1854 left the army and settled on his estate near Vienna, devoting himself to the study of natural history. He married Elizabeth Farquharson, the daughter of a Scottish general. She was only twenty years old when she married Karl, who was fifty-six. She was intelligent and lively and a convert to Catholicism.

Friedrich was the oldest of the couple's three children. He was brought up at home—first in Florence, eventually in England—where he received a thorough but varied education at the hands of several tutors. He never took a university degree.

Friedrich's father died when he was eighteen years old. Soon after, he contracted a severe case of typhus, from which he almost died and which left him partially deaf. At this time, while in Vienna, he also had a psychological crisis from which he emerged with "his moral will and religious convictions" reinforced. He met a Dutch Dominican, Father Raymond Hocking, who was very helpful to him, and later, in Paris, he met the Abbé Huvelin, who, according to Hügel's biographer Maurice Nedoncelle, "influenced him more than anyone."[55] Huvelin was a renowned spiritual director in Paris at that time and an obvious father figure. He was, according to Hügel, "a rich and deep, a cultivated, above all an heroic soul, to whom I owe incalculably much."[56] Nedoncelle says of Huvelin that he was "Naturally sympathetic, [and] treated every personality with respect; severe with no one but himself."[57]

Baron von Hügel is best known for his many works on the mystical aspects of Catholic life, among them *The Eternal Life* (1912), *The Reality of God* and *Religion and Agnosticism* (published together posthumously in 1931).

G.K. Chesterton (1874-1936)

Gilbert Keith Chesterton was born into a comfortable middle-class family in London. His younger brother, Cecil, called Gilbert's childhood "the happiest in litera- ture." G.K. became a major Christian apologist even before his conversion to Catholicism. Two of his most influen- tial works are *Orthodoxy* and *The Everlasting Man*.

Chesterton's father, Edward, was known in the fam- ily by the affectionate name of "Mister" or "Mister Ed." He was described by G.K. as "serene, humorous and full of hobbies"[58] and by his daughter-in-law as "a man of many small and endearing talents."[59] Although nominally the head of the Chesterton real estate firm, Edward, in part because of a health problem and in part because of a lack of interest in business, spent most of his time at home with his wife and children and in the expression of his many avocations, which included, but were not limited to, "water-color painting, making models, photography, collecting stained glass, fretwork, magic lanterns and me- dieval illuminations."[60] Mister Ed was described personally as being even-tempered and having good sense "tinged with dreaminess" and stable, loyal relationships with other people.

His mother was also a major figure in young Ches- terton's life, and in many respects had a stronger character than her husband. To Cecil—the two boys were quite close—the mother was quite simply "the cleverest woman in London."[61]

Tragedy struck the family when Gilbert was three years old: His older and much-adored sister Beatrice died of illness at the age of eight, and he never forgot the sorrow of her loss. The parents were also devastated; indeed, G.K.'s otherwise merry father was never able to mention her name again.

The Chestertons were nominal Christians. Formal church attendance appears to have been limited to attendance at Bedford Chapel, where Stopford Brooke preached. Brooke had left the Anglican Church, and Bedford Chapel was Unitarian. Alzina Stone Dale and Joseph Pearce note that Chesterton's parents "were 'freethinkers' in the best Victorian tradition, paying lip-service to a Unitarian form of worship and thus rejecting 'the formularies of the Church of England.'"[62] According to Cecil, his parents believed in "the fatherhood of God, the brotherhood of man, the non-eternity of evil, the final salvation of souls."[63] In short, theirs was an optimistic, upbeat, rather humanistic religion, with an emphasis on ethics.

With regard to G.K.'s relationship with his father, Pearce quotes a childhood friend of Chesterton's to the effect that "he had never met 'with greater kindliness'— to say nothing of other sterling qualities—than that of the father, the businessman whose feeling for literature and all beautiful things worked so much upon his sons in childhood."[64] In particular, Edward Chesterton was extremely well-read and passed on his love of English literature to G.K. who knew a great deal of it by heart:

"Mister Ed was the most important person in Gilbert's childhood; he became his small son's habitual companion, able to spend much of his time at home since his weak heart had allowed him to retire."[65]

Michael Coren, in *Gilbert: The Man Who was G. K. Chesterton* confirms the relationship between father and son: "The two men were close, friends as well as father and son." Coren quotes from a letter from G.K. to Ronald Knox, written just before the elder Chesterton's death: "My father is the very best man I ever knew of that generation that never understood the new need of a spiritual authority; and lives perfectly by the sort of religion men had when rationalism was rational."[66] And as he wrote of his own childhood:

> I am sorry if the landscape or the people appear disappointingly respectable and even reasonable, and deficient in all those unpleasant qualities that make a biography really popular. I regret that I have no gloomy and savage father to offer to the public gaze as the true cause of all my tragic heritage; no pale-faced and partially poisoned mother whose suicidal instincts have cursed me with the temptations of the artistic temperament. I regret that there was nothing in the range of our family much more racy than a remote and mildly impecunious uncle; and that I cannot do my duty as a true modern, by cursing everybody who made me whatever I am. I am not clear about what that is; but I am pretty sure that most of it is my own fault. And I am compelled to confess that I look back to that landscape of my first days with a pleasure that should doubtless be reserved for the Utopias of the Futurist.[67]

Albert Schweitzer (1875-1965)

Albert Schweitzer was a famous theologian and a prominent musician and organist whose writings on ethics were
also well-known. But to most people he is best known
as a physician-missionary in Equatorial Africa.

His childhood seems to have been extremely happy,
and he was quite aware that he had been granted an especially happy youth: "I felt this happy youth even as
something oppressive."[68] In a sense, he suffered from a
kind of guilt because of his fortunate background and
family. As a child, he refused to wear clothing that would
set him apart from the other, less fortunate children in
his school. It seems reasonable to assume that even his
missionary work was in some respects to share something
of his own good fortune with others.

He lived with his father and mother who were both
devoted to him, growing up in a cultured German Christian home. His father was pastor of a Protestant church
and was much respected in the community. Even before
Albert went to school, his father began to teach him music
on an old piano. When he was eight years old, his father gave him a New Testament, which he read eagerly.
Somewhat later, when he was around eleven or twelve,
he lived with his Uncle Louis and Aunt Sophie in order
that he could attend the nearby gymnasium (German high
school) at Mulhausen. Theirs was a strict household, and
Albert missed his home: "In my first years at Mulhausen,
I suffered much from a homesick longing for the church
at Gunsbach; I missed my father's sermons and the services I had been familiar with all my life."[69]

He also mentions that his family was saved from

money worries thanks to an inheritance from a distant relative of his mother's. The result was that, "during my last years at school there was again unclouded sunshine over my home. We were all in good health and lived in the closest harmony together. The relations between parents and children were ideal, thanks to the wise understanding with which the former treated us even in our follies. . . . [My parents] trained us for freedom. . . . My father was my dearest friend."[70]

Martin Buber (1878-1965)

Martin Buber was a Jewish theologian who emphasized the personal relationship of the believer with God and with others. His most famous book is *I and Thou.*

Buber was born in Vienna and lived as a small child with his parents in a house overlooking the Danube River. The pleasant certainty of his first three years was shattered when his "mother literally disappeared without leaving a trace, and the home of his childhood was broken up."[71] Martin, an only child, was sent to live with his paternal grandparents, Solomon and Adele, who lived on a large estate near Lvov in the Austrian crownland of Galacia. He never learned from his grandparents what had happened to his mother, and at first, he apparently expected at any moment to see her again. One event that occurred shortly after his arrival at his grandparents' is of special importance:

> Once, when he was not yet four, the boy stood on this balcony [a balcony in his grandparents' house] with a girl several years older, the daughter of a

neighbor whom his grandmother had asked to look after him. They both leaned on the railing, and here there took place the dialogue that had not taken place with his grandparents. "I cannot remember that I spoke of my mother to my older comrade," Buber related. "But I still hear how the big girl said to me: 'No, she will never come back.'" He remained silent, but he had no doubt that she had spoken the truth.[72]

Martin's experience on the balcony was the decisive one of his life, "the one without which neither his early seeking for unity nor his later focus on dialogue and on the meeting with the 'eternal Thou' is understandable."[73]

Whatever the impact of the loss of his mother, Martin had a strong and loving grandfather and a strong and loving substitute-mother in his grandmother Buber: "Despite the many activities of business and scholarship that absorbed Solomon Buber, he found time to be something of a companion to his gifted grandson. If it was his grandmother, Adele, who taught him the true love of reading and of language, it was his grandfather who, even after Martin had gone back to live with his father, introduced him to the world of scholarship and, what was more important, to the task of Hebrew translation, which was to occupy Martin throughout his life."[74]

Buber's father, who had remarried, reentered Martin's life again when the boy was eight. The boy went to join his father and his stepmother every summer on his father's estate. At fourteen he moved from his grandfather's home to his father's townhouse.

Although the impact of his mother's loss affected him

all his life, Buber was sustained at the time and in later years by the love of a grandfather and a grandmother, and as a child he was reunited with his father.

Karl Barth (1886-1968)

Karl Barth, the great Swiss-German Protestant theologian of the first half of the twentieth century, is probably best known for the founding of a neo-orthodox theology, that is, a powerfully argued reaction against the liberal Protestant theology that had emerged with such vigor in the nineteenth century. Among his important works are *Commentary on Romans, Credo, The Word of God and the Word of Man*, and his twelve-volume *Church Dogmatics*.

Barth fits the hypothesis well. He was born into long lines of German Reformed pastors and intellectuals on both sides of his family. He was the eldest of five children. A younger brother, Peter, was his first, and for many years his closest, friend. Karl's father, Johann Friedrich (Fritz), was a prominent pastor, first in Berne and then in several other towns in Switzerland.

Barth was close to his father, who ordained him in the Protestant Cathedral in Berne in 1908, when Karl was twenty-two. One of Karl's brothers was also ordained by their father. Fritz Barth died rather suddenly from blood poisoning in 1912, when he was only fifty-five years old:

> Karl hastened to his father's death-bed immediately after his Sunday sermon. [Barth's biographer now quotes Barth himself] "He said farewell to his loved ones peacefully. One of his last remarks which we could hear, spoken as though to students in a lec-

ture room, was: 'The main thing is not scholarship, nor learning, nor criticism, but to love the Lord Jesus. We need a living relationship with God, and we must ask the Lord for that.'".... Karl ... gave a moving sermon in Safenwil the following Sunday on the occasion of his father's death. And it may well be said that only from this point on did he really begin to see and to understand what his father stood for, since during his student days he had had many reservations about his views.[75]

Karl followed in his father's footsteps—even taking a position in one of the little towns where his father had once served years before.

Dietrich Bonhoeffer (1906-1945)

Dietrich and his twin sister were born into a large German family, the sixth and seventh of eight children. They lived in a large and pleasant house in Breslau, Germany, where their father was professor of psychiatry and neurology and director of a hospital for nervous diseases. Their loving and intelligent mother kept family life organized and stimulating, giving Dietrich his religious instruction by reading Bible stories and providing moral commentary. She also had a talent for painting and a love of music. Dietrich's father came from a respected family of theologians, doctors, and lawyers: "This outstanding heredity brought him distinguished parents, gifted brothers and sisters, and a home in which tradition and originality combined to create an altogether exceptional atmosphere of creative vigour. Few indeed come into the world with such a commanding prospect of a happy life. None could then have imagined the future in which that life would end."[76]

From 1912, his father held a chair of neurology and psychiatry in Berlin. His father, like his mother, was a major presence in the lives of all the children. Dietrich's twin later wrote that their father "showed his respect for warm-hearted, unselfish and disciplined actions and relied on us to stand by the weak."[77] In spite of his busy schedule their father was present at all meals, and he treated his children with respect and affection. [78]

Dietrich was blond, energetic and athletic; he was a talented musician, though not enough to be a professional. By fourteen, he had already showed an interest in theology and a deeply religious character, which set him very much apart from most of his school and college friends. Yet his father was not a believer—rather, an "agnostic-humanist"—and his older brothers were naturalistic skeptics. There were often heated discussions, but no estrangements. Nevertheless, Dietrich's mother saw that the family celebrated religious holidays such as Christmas, Easter, and Pentecost, and she supported Dietrich's growing religious involvement.

The Bonhoeffer family was generally what could be called "liberal" in the best sense of the word—cultured, open, concerned for others, hopeful about the Weimar government after World War I, and opposed to fascism. Dietrich strongly opposed the Nazis, and Hitler in particular. Found to be part of the plot on Hitler's life, he was executed very near the end of World War II, in the spring of 1945. Although his life ended early, his letters and his book, *The Cost of Discipleship*, are recognized as

Christian classics. His respect for his loving and impressive father lasted to Dietrich's death.[79]

Abraham Heschel (1907-1972)

Abraham Heschel is famous primarily for his great books *Man is Not Alone, The Earth is the Lord's,* and *Guide for the Perplexed,* as well as for other books on Jewish philosophy and mysticism.

Heschel was born in Warsaw, Poland, descended from an illustrious line of Hasidic rabbis from the Ukrainian town of Mezbizh, where the Baal Shem Tov, the founder of the Hasidic movement, had lived the last years of his life. His grandfather Heschel, for whom he was named, had been the last great rebbe of Mezbizh. Heschel's biographer, Samuel Dresner, notes that "even from early childhood [Abraham] was viewed with great expectations. At the age of four or five, scholars would place him on a table and interrogate him for the surprising and amusing answers he would give. When his father died during his tenth year, there were those who wanted the boy to succeed him [as rabbi] almost at once."[80]

Even before his father's death, Abraham saw himself as having two major Hasidic masters whom he took as lifetime models and spiritual fathers. As he himself put it,

> The earliest fascination I can recall is associated with the Baal Shem, whose parables disclosed some of the first insights I gained as a child. He remained a model too sublime to follow, yet too overwhelming to ignore.

It was in my ninth year that the presence of Reb
Menahem Mendl of Kotzk, known as the Kotzker,
entered my life. Since then he has remained a steady
companion and a haunting challenge. . . . Years later
I realized that, in being guided by both the Baal
Shem Tov and the Kotzker, I had allowed two forces
to carry on a struggle within me. . . . The one re-
minded me that there could be a Heaven on earth,
the other shocked me into discovering Hell in the
alleged Heavenly places in our world.[81]

We can see that from his early youth, Heschel felt
influenced by male models on whom he patterned his life;
he saw himself as part of the tradition of great Hasidic
thinkers. The loss of his own father was clearly palli-
ated by the presence in his youth of Hasidic masters.

To ANYONE WHO KNOWS THE HISTORY of modern philosophy and theology, the figures treated in this chapter
make a very representative list of the prominent defend-
ers of belief in God. These are many of the major theists from the seventeenth to the twentieth century: Blaise
Pascal, George Berkeley, Bishop Butler, Thomas Reid,
Edmund Burke, Moses Mendelssohn, William Paley, William and Samuel Wilberforce, François Chateaubriand,
Friedrich Schleiermacher, John Henry Cardinal Newman,
Alexis de Tocqueville, Sören Kierkegaard, Baron von
Hügel, G. K. Chesterton, Albert Schweitzer, Martin Buber,
Karl Barth, Dietrich Bonhoeffer, Abraham Heschel. In
the case of Butler, biographical information is limited. But
otherwise the preceding list is one of *clearly positive*

father-son relationships—or of good father-substitute-and -son relationships. There is only one case of serious estrangement, Kierkegaard's, which was resolved in a way that provides direct support for the present hypothesis. Kierkegaard's reconciliation with his father led the great Danish thinker to express an understanding of how the father complex is related to belief in God.

4

Extensions and Qualifications

THE CONTROL GROUP of prominent theorists presented in the previous chapter lived during the
same time period as the famous atheists; ten were
English, three French, four German, three Jewish, and one
Danish. All told, the early childhoods of these twenty-one
important thinkers are remarkable for their support of my
hypothesis: there is no early death of a father, no abandonment, no dramatic rejection by the father. Still less
are there other forms of obvious abuse from fathers among
these cases. This picture is in marked contrast with the
atheist sample.

Nevertheless, human lives are complex, and we should
not expect a single hypothesis to account for all relevant
cases, though I am rather surprised at the high number
of cases that this single theory does seem to explain. We
now need to address qualifications and exceptions.

SUBSTITUTE FATHERS

The original statement of my hypothesis referred specifically to the biological father of the child. One obvious way in which this can be qualified is if the child had a substitute father, that is, another man who filled the fatherly role in a significant way. In such cases, the hypothesis predicts that the tendency to atheism should be markedly reduced or even eliminated. In order to explicate this issue in some detail, we will look at the lives of two important religious figures, Don Bosco and Hilaire Belloc, and one contemporary literary figure, Walker Percy.

Don Bosco (1815-1888)

We begin with Don Bosco. His real name was John Melchior Bosco ("Don" is a title of honor). He was born in a small hamlet in northern Italy, not too far from Turin. His mother and father were both from local peasant stock. John's father, a poor farmer, died when John was two years old. There was an older stepbrother from a previous marriage of his father's, and a younger brother as well. The entire burden of caring for this family fell on John's mother, Margaret. John's childhood was physically very hard. He drew water from the well, chopped firewood, cleaned the cowshed, and when he got a little older began digging, weeding, and ploughing on nearby farms to help support the family. From his early childhood, John showed intelligence, a strong character, and an outgoing personality. His mother was pious and, though she could not read and write, knew much Bible history and many prayers. Young John learned his prayers, actively practiced them, and excelled at encouraging other people to pray with him. As a boy, he was very good at such tricks as tight-rope walking, somersaults, trials of strength, and the like, and when a crowd would gather around to watch him, he would ask them to pay for the show by reciting with him the Our Father or the Hail Mary.[1]

John's older half-brother, Anthony, was often hostile to him. One might assume that having lost his father, and with a hateful older brother, John was, despite his pious mother, a perfect candidate for atheism or some form of religious or social rebellion. But we know that several important men came into John Bosco's life in his early teens. One was a maternal uncle; the others were priests.[2]

In the autumn of 1828, when John was thirteen, his mother's brother appeared on the scene to help him escape Anthony's dominion and to pursue his studies and the priesthood. Early on John had learned how to read, though it is not clear how or from whom, and he continued his studies under Don Calosso, a local priest, of whom John later said, "No one could ever have imagined it. Don Calosso was for me a real angel of the Lord. I loved him more than a father. I prayed for him constantly, it was a pleasure to do what I could for him."[3] Don Calosso, a somewhat elderly priest, died when John was fifteen, in November of 1830.

John's obvious need for a new father figure was met briefly by a priest named Dassano, who took on young John and gave him lessons in Latin. But soon John developed a friendship with another father figure—a relationship that lasted for many years—a priest named Don Cafasso. John often went to seek his advice. This priest, along with several others, paid for John's seminary studies which began in 1835, when John was twenty.

After his ordination, John went on to the Ecclesiastical College at Turin to study theology. While he was in the College, he began his work—for which he is famous—with young boys. The orphans in and around Turin were products of the early Industrial Revolution. Anyone who has read Dickens knows about the harsh life of such children at this time. John's good-natured charity and his deep spirituality quickly made him a favorite with these boys, and he gathered a hundred of them or more. Later, he founded the Salesian Order, devoted to meeting the spiritual, social, educationa,l and physical needs of such children. This boy, who had had important substitute fathers in his own life, became a father figure—a substitute father—to thousands of other boys. (Under Don Bosco's encouragement, a similar order of nuns was also founded to address the needs of girls.)

One might ask how young John fared between the age of two, when his father died, and the age of thirteen, when he first met an obvious father figure. There was, of course, the maternal uncle who rescued him from Anthony. There is certainly evidence that the issue of a father was important to him during his childhood. For example, his very earliest contacts with priests were disappointing. He respected them from a distance: "He greeted them, but they passed him by without a word, without a sign. Later he complained: 'I used to cry about this and I told my friends that if ever I became a priest, I would not behave like that. I would talk to the boys, and say a good word and give them advice.'"[4]

He did have one father-figure even then, however: when John was nine years old, he had the first of many dreams in which Christ appeared to him. These dreams were very important in his life, and over a hundred of them are in the historical record. The first of them, at this early time of John's life, was a dream in which he was fighting with some other young boys. Jesus appeared to him in the dream and told him to stop fighting and to win the boys over with love.[5] The Virgin also appeared in the dream and said to John: "You did not know it but you were fighting with wolves. Go amongst them with courage, and they will change into lambs. This will be your vocation later on."[6] Young John understood this dream to mean that he was to become a priest. Because of his personal sanctity, his charity, and other qualities, John Bosco was canonized in 1934.

Hilaire Belloc (1870-1953)[7]

Hilaire Belloc was a novelist, a writer of verse, and a brilliant and opinionated popular historian. He was also one of the great champions of Catholicism in the first half of the twentieth century. He was born to a French father—Louis Belloc, a painter—and an English mother. Hilaire's mother, Bessie Parkes, was thirty-eight when she married—quite late for those days. Bessie came from a prominent family of unenthusiastic Unitarians, but her father had been active in the Liberal Party. Bessie lost her Unitarian faith while, as a young woman, she was translating David Strauss's skeptical *Life of Jesus*. Nevertheless, she converted to Catholicism some years later. She and Louis Belloc were married in 1867 in a Catholic church in London. The young couple was wealthy: Bessie's father owned three impressive houses and a large collection of Italian paintings. The Bellocs were extremely well-matched and very happy together. They divided the year between La Celle St. Cloud in France (just outside

Paris) and Wimpole Street in London. Their first child was a daughter, Marie, born in 1868. (In her day, she was a famous writer of more than forty crime novels.) Hilaire, the Bellocs' second and last child, came two years later. In the summer of 1872 Louis Belloc fell gravely ill and died in August of that year at the age of forty-two. Little Hilaire, aged two, was at the funeral holding his mother's hand.

As A. N. Wilson has observed, "Hilaire Belloc was to grow up without any men in his immediate family. All the women close to him, moreover, his mother and his two grandmothers, were widows."[8] In the late 1870s, Bessie lost a substantial amount of her inherited wealth through unfortunate speculation by the broker to whom she had entrusted it. Henceforth, all his life Belloc would be in financial straits.

Belloc attended a small Catholic school called the Oratory whose headmaster was the great John Henry Cardinal Newman. Interestingly enough, Newman was a very distant figure as far as Belloc was concerned, and Belloc seems not to have been particularly impressed by him. He was certainly no father figure for Hilaire. At age seventeen, Belloc left the Oratory.

The father-figure that Belloc did find was no less than Henry Edward Cardinal Manning of London. When Bessie had returned to England after Louis's funeral, she immediately called on the Cardinal, who some years earlier had been instrumental in her conversion and for whom she had deep admiration. Manning understood her grief: while the Anglican archdeacon at Chichester, before his conversion to Catholicism, he too had been widowed. As a young child Belloc was blessed by Manning and at least once heard him preach.[9] In his late teens, Hilaire began to establish a close relationship with the Cardinal:

> It was my custom during my first days in London, as a very young man, before I went to Oxford, to call upon the Cardinal as regularly as he would receive me; and during those brief interviews I heard from him many things which I have had later occasions to test by the experience of human life. I was, it may be said, too young to judge things so deep as sanctity and wisdom; but, on the other hand, youth has vision, especially upon elemental things; and Manning did seem to me (and still seems to me) much the greatest Englishman of his time. . . . He never admitted the possibility of compromise between Catholic and non-Catholic society. He perceived the necessary conflict and gloried in it.[10]

Belloc was clearly deeply influenced by Manning; in particular, Belloc, too, gloried in a militant Catholicism and in conflict.

Walker Percy (1916-1990)[11]

Percy, like Samuel Butler, wrote both fiction and philosophy, but will likely be remembered most for his fiction. Trained as a physician, he contracted tuberculosis in his first years of practice and was unable to continue work as a doctor. He wrote such acclaimed novels as *The Moviegoer* (1961), *Lancelot* (1977), and *The Thanatos Syndrome* (1987), as well as nonfiction works dealing with language theory and other aspects of philosophy and contemporary culture, such as *The Message in the Bottle* (1975) and *Lost in the Cosmos* (1983).

Percy lost his father and his grandfather early in his life. His grandfather shot himself when Percy was only a year old. It was never determined whether this shooting was an accident or suicide. Walker's parents—his father was LeRoy and his mother Mattie Sue—had two other boys in addition to Walker. The Percys were considered a happy family until the father's depression declared itself. In 1925, when Walker was nine years old, his father spent a few weeks in a psychiatric clinic for depression, and at some point around that time he tried to commit suicide by cutting his wrists. He continued to suffer from serious depression. A few years later, while Walker and one of his brothers were away at summer camp, their father shot himself with a double-barreled shotgun in the attic of the family home. Walker was thirteen at the time; his father was forty-four.

Mattie Sue Percy and her sons were now on their own and Walker's biographer says that for all of them "the pain of loss would never go away."[12] Many of Percy's novels contain references to suicide and reflections on the idea of the "lost father."

Soon after her husband's death, Mrs. Percy took her boys to live with relatives. Several months later, LeRoy's bachelor cousin, Will, invited Percy's mother and her sons to live with him, and so it was that the thirteen-year-old Walker came to meet and get to know his forty-five-year-old "Uncle Will" who was, in addition to being a lawyer, a decorated infantry officer from World War I, and a published poet. This invitation marked a major turning point in Walker Percy's life.

Percy said that he gained from this friendship with the older man "a vocation and in a real sense a second self, that is, the work and the self which, for better or worse, would not otherwise have been open to me.[13] Percy said that Uncle Will gave him, his two brothers, and his mother "a complete articulated view of the world as tragic as it was noble. I was to be introduced to Shakespeare, to Keats, to Brahms, to Beethoven."[14]

For his part, Uncle Will, in a book that he published in 1941, gave his own views on the relationships he had voluntarily taken on: "My favorite cousin, LeRoy Percy, died two months before Mother's death, and his brave and beautiful wife, Mattie Sue Phinizy, two years after Father's. Their three boys, Walker, LeRoy and Phiniz, came to live with me and I adopted them as my sons. . . . Suddenly my household was filled with youth, and suddenly I found myself unprepared, with the responsibility of directing young lives in a world that was changing and that seemed to me on the threshold of chaos."[15]

Walker always felt that Will "was the most extraordinary man" he had ever met, and though he did not use the word "love" in this context, Walker felt that he owed Will an unpayable debt.[16]

Walker's mother would sometimes encourage the boys to go to the Presbyterian Sunday school, but they stopped going once there was no pressure to do so.[17] Percy considered that neither Presbyterianism nor the Episcopal Church had the answers for him, and in his youth he considered himself irreligious. Will, who had once professed Roman Catholicism, maintained a certain affection for it, but was apparently non-practicing.

In 1931, when Walker was fifteen, his mother died when the car she was driving went off a bridge. Percy apparently believed that his mother's death had been suicide, like that of his father. After this devastating second death, Walker and his brothers looked to Uncle Will for their total support, which he gave without reserve. Will was a caring and a careful guardian. He read to the boys, organized vacation trips, and in due course, after the boys had agreed to the proposal, formally adopted all three boys.[18]

When Walker was twenty-six, Uncle Will died of cardiovascular disease at age fifty-six. When Walker called one of his brothers to tell him the bad news, his brother said, "I feel adrift. The anchor is gone. I never saw Uncle Will do a selfish thing. I can't say that about anybody else I've ever known."[19] Walker dedicated his award-winning first novel, *The Moviegoer*, to "Uncle Will *In Memoriam*."

At age thirty, Walker Percy married. He and his wife, Bunt, converted to Catholicism, adopted a daughter, had another, and in time became grandparents. Walker Percy's religious beliefs were deeply held and well known; they explicitly informed many of his essays and, implicitly, much of his fiction.

IF WE LOOK BACK at the theists discussed in the previous chapter, we recall several important father-figures in their lives as well. Edmund Burke was close to his maternal uncles, especially Garret, and to his school-master Shackleton; William Wilberforce was close to his paternal uncle and revered John Newton almost as a father. There was also Father Huvelin for von Hügel, Buber's grandfather, Heschel's teachers, and Tocqueville's Abbé Lesueur.

By contrast, we saw no such father figures in the lives of Hume, Meslier, Nietzsche, Russell, Sartre, Schopenhauer, d'Alembert, Feuerbach, Freud, and most of the other atheists. Voltaire's Jesuit teachers can be seen as minor substitute fathers, and perhaps this is why Voltaire remained a deist and never became a true atheist. There is the hint of a possible substitute father in the life of Camus—but again, perhaps this is why Camus was more a reluctant than a militant atheist. In short, the presence of a positive and effective father, or father-figure, seems to be a strong antidote to atheism.

POLITICAL ATHEISTS

One possible extension of the thesis is to suggest that a defective father was also important in the lives of political figures especially known for their hostility to religion— in particular, Christianity and Judaism. Three such figures immediately come to mind: Joseph Stalin, Adolf Hitler, and Mao Zedong.

Joseph Stalin (1879-1953)

Perhaps the simplest summary of Stalin's relationship to his father is the following comment made by a friend who knew Stalin during his early years: "Undeserved and severe beatings made the boy as hard and heartless as the father was. Since all people in authority over others seemed to him to be like his father, there soon arose in him a vengeful feeling against all people standing above him."[20] In addition, his father was often not at home, spending some years working at various jobs in nearby towns. He drank heavily and beat his wife, Joseph's mother, to whom Joseph was attached. This rough and violent father had great difficulty making a living, and wanted his son to become a cobbler or a factory worker. Young Stalin suffered other childhood traumas as well. He nearly died from smallpox, which left his face pock-marked; his left arm was permanently injured as the result of a childhood accident. His parents were both peasants who were born serfs and were probably illiterate.

Joseph's mother gave her son—her only surviving child—her deep affection and support and apparently kept his father from breaking the boy's spirit. She pushed her son toward the priesthood in the Orthodox Church, and for a few years Stalin studied in a seminary. Nevertheless, in the seminary he became a strong atheist.[21] Stalin's family name was Djugashvili; he later rejected his name and changed it to the Russian word for "steel."

As a political leader, Stalin persecuted the Orthodox Church in particular with great vigor; the Communists murdered thousands of Orthodox priests, often in gruesome ways. And in view of Stalin's character, it is not difficult to understand why communism, with its explicit rejection of God and all other higher authorities, such as the Tsar, had great appeal for him.

Adolf Hitler (1889-1945)

Like Stalin, young Adolf received severe and regular beatings from his father. Alois Hitler is described as "authoritarian and selfish, and showing little concern for the feelings of his much younger wife and little understanding of his children,"[22] and as a "hard, unsympathetic and

short-tempered man."[23] Adolf had an older half-brother
from an earlier marriage of his father, also Alois, who
bitterly complained that his father often beat him "un-
mercifully."[24] There are a number of other stories about
the violence of Adolf's father, which included severe
beatings of the family dog, and which also extended to
his mother.

Adolf's older stepbrother ran away from home at fourteen, never to return during his father's lifetime. Adolf
appears, then, to have caught the brunt of his father's
hostility. His older half sister, Paula, reported that Adolf
"got his sound thrashing every day."[25] On the other hand,
Adolf's mother, Clara, who had three children who died
very young, before Adolf was born, lavished affection on
Adolf, and he always had fond memories of his mother.
Though Hitler rarely talked about his family, it is clear
that he did not get along with his father.

When his father died, Adolf was fourteen, and from
that time on had no father-figure at all. His mother, like
Stalin's mother, pushed her son toward the church. For
a few years, he went along with this, but by the age of
confirmation he was clearly rebellious, and from that time
on never had anything good to say about Christianity. His
attitude toward Judaism is, of course, well known. Nevertheless, he did retain a modest, if rather abstract, belief in God.

Hitler was deeply influenced by two atheist philosophers—Schopenhauer and Nietzsche. He could quote the
former by the page and often referred to the latter.[26] Like
all politicians, however, he was mostly concerned with
power, and his primary interest in these two philosophers
arose from their emphasis on the human will. His deep

hostility to Christianity arose from its Jewish origin, its social power, and, I would argue, its portrayal of God as Father. .

Mao Zedong (1893-1976)

Mao may never have been especially hostile to Christianity or to the idea of God the Father, since they were absent from his Chinese upbringing. But the appeal to Mao of a revolutionary and atheistic philosophy would have been strong because of his relationship with his father. Mao's father is described as a family tyrant, and from childhood young Mao sided with his mother and other members of the family in implicit rebellions. He clearly hated his father and learned his first appreciation of revolution and rebellion in his own family setting.

POLITICAL ATHEISM of extreme kinds does not provide clear examples of the defective father hypothesis since, as noted, most politicians are primarily concerned with obtaining power rather than rejecting God in an intellectual way. Still, there is reason to see the relevance of the defective father hypothesis to the appeal of atheistic violence in their lives.

THE ATHEIST FATHER AS A POSITIVE INFLUENCE

There is another obvious source of atheism—namely, when it is directly taught by a father who is loved and admired by his child. Probably the best-known case of this type is that of James Mill (1773-1836) and John Stuart Mill

(1806-1873). James Mill, though a philosopher, historian, and economist of some importance in his own right, is nonetheless better known as the father of his son. James, as a young man, studied in philosophy and divinity and obtained a license to preach. He became an atheist, according to his son, because he believed there was too much evil in the world to justify belief in an infinitely good God.

James was his son's devoted tutor. John Stuart was almost completely homeschooled by his father who provided, as one historian of philosophy has put it, "one of the most formidable educations on record."[27] John started Greek at age three, Latin at eight, and by fourteen he had read most of the Greek and Latin classics, read widely in history, and studied mathematics and logic intensively. In the course of his education, John Stuart embraced the philosophical radicalism of his father and of his father's associate Jeremy Bentham. Years later, John Stuart concluded that his education had been too much based on analytic thought, at the expense of his emotional life: poetry and literature had been neglected. Nevertheless, John Stuart remained throughout his life very much in the general school of philosophical and social thought represented by his father.

Curiously, John Stuart's posthumously published writings on religion show that his rejection of God was less intense than had been assumed during his lifetime. In the last of his *Three Essays on Religion* (1874), he makes some significant concessions to the arguments and evidence for the supernatural view of religion.

We have in this famous father-and-son pair evidence of the powerful effect of the direct teaching of atheism, combined with the son's identification with his father. This generational continuity is part of any normal education and occurred in Mill's case in the same manner as other fathers transmit a belief in God to their children. John Stuart Mill's atheism, therefore, was not a result of psychological traumas having to do with a defective father.

Nevertheless, it is possible that a good father who taught his child atheism would nevertheless inadvertently be a model for a benevolent Father-God. Thus, we might expect the children of good atheist fathers often to find themselves leaning toward or even converting to theism. Our discussion is focused on atheists with bad fathers, who show the same dynamic in reverse.

MEN AND WOMEN: SOME DIFFERENCES

As I mentioned in the introduction, there are reasons to believe that men and women often have a different psychology lying behind their rejection of God. So far, the prominent atheists we have discussed have all been men. The sole exception has been Madalyn Murray O'Hair; her intense atheism, however, seems to have followed the pattern typical of males. I will develop this proposed difference between men and women before turning to the evidence for it.

Though the major psychological *origin* of intense atheism is very likely the same for both sexes (a defective father), their *responses* after they have rejected the Jewish or Christian God are quite different. For men, God seems to function primarily as a *principle* of justice and order in the world—and only secondarily as a person with whom one has a relationship. In other words, God's law and providential control seem to be the central aspects of belief for men. For women, by contrast, it is their *relationship* with God which is primary, while God as a principle of justice and order, though important, is typically seen as secondary.

We would expect, therefore, that men who become atheists will find a new absolute principle with which to order the world. Thus, we expect male atheists to be quite explicitly atheistic and to have a new "divinity" that takes the intellectual place of God. As a consequence, atheistic men should be intense believers in such alternative principles as reason, science, progress, humanism, socialism, communism, or existentialism. And this is what we see in the the lives of atheists. Bertrand Russell's daughter was quite aware of his search for certainty in mathematics as a religiously-motivated substitute for God. The French revolutionary atheists (or, occasionally, serious skeptics) sought a similar substitute for God in their deification of Reason: they even put a female statue in the Cathedral of Notre Dame in Paris representing the goddess reason. Many atheists today are well known as believers in science: they treat science as a worldview or personal philosophy, not just as an important methodology and type of knowledge. Marxists and communists are famous for interpreting their ideology as an absolute system, for which they fanatically evangelize. Many ideologues persecute "non-believers" in a way that makes the Inquisition look insignificant.

In the case of women, the vacuum created by loss of the divine relationship is filled by other relationships. The woman who rejects God will look for substitute relationships in some new enthusiasm. For example, many contemporary feminists adamantly reject God, interpreting the Jewish and Christian God as "patriarchal," by which they mean that a relationship with God is interpreted as oppressive for women, and therefore unacceptable. It is not the idea of a god per se that they reject; rather, the god of a particular relationship. They want to redefine the relationship. As a result, their new enthusiasm—in this case, feminism—should offer important new relationships to take the place of God the Father. Feminism is well-known for its redefinition of God as female: the Goddess, or God the Mother. Such women are not so much atheists in the strict sense of the word as redefiners of the highest and most sublime kind of relationship.

Furthermore, we should expect women, in developing an ideological substitute for God as male, as Father, to emphasize *female relationships in this world* as well. Lesbianism, so common among feminists, and the feminist emphasis on "sisterhood," can be seen as flowing philosophically from the rejection of divine patriarchy. It is the expression in this world—in the horizontal interpersonal realm—of the position that feminists have taken with regard to the vertical dimension of belief in a matriarchal god.

It is also likely that some kinds of religious "scandal" are more likely to offend men and others, women. We can predict that women will find interpersonal abuse, betrayal, or abandonment by male religious figures (ranging from their fathers, to teachers, ministers, priests, and rabbis) far more disturbing on average than would men. By contrast, men would be more disturbed at fathers who are weak or unprincipled, at religious or church hypocrisy—at the failure of principle. Thus, theological controversies should be, relatively speaking, more of a masculine preoccupation, while controversies over church policies as they affect lives directly should have a stronger impact on women. Such differences in vulnerability to different types of theological or religious failure suggest that some events are more likely to precipitate atheism in men than in women.

The distinction between males' greater involvement in God as a principle and females' greater concern with God as relationship is consistent with Carol Gilligan's well-known position on the differences between male and female moral reasoning.[28] She has provided considerable evidence that women more often tend to focus on the interpersonal consequences of a moral dilemma, and men more on the abstract principles involved in the dilemma. Women see the maintenance of satisfactory relationships as of special importance, emphasizing mercy, while men are much more concerned with the integrity of abstract ideas such as justice. Other feminists, along with Gilligan, have proposed that relationships are a more important part of female psychological identity than of male identity.[29]

The female emphasis on relationships shows itself very early in life. Compared to boys, girl babies attend earlier and more reliably to the human face; they are more soothed by words and song; they speak earlier; they pay more attention to people than to objects; they are more aware of emotional communication. Even at two to four days of age, baby girls maintain more eye contact with adults than do baby boys. These biases in favor of the interpersonal endure throughout life. Girls show more empathy with the distress of others than do boys. Such empathy has been identified as a central component in the development of moral behavior.[30]

Our concern with male and female differences is not to imply that all men and all women fit the proposed pattern. Obviously, both aspects of God—his principled and his interpersonal natures—are important in some degree to each sex. I would guess that the proposed dichotomy adequately characterizes 60 to 70 percent of each sex. Hence, there remain many men and women who will better fit the pattern of the opposite sex.

We now turn to look at evidence in the lives of contemporary feminists, which bears on the preceding discussion.

Simone de Beauvoir (1908-1986)

Simone de Beauvoir is certainly one of the best-known women intellectuals of the twentieth century. She was a woman of letters, a disciple of Jean-Paul Sartre, and a feminist thinker in her own right. Her book *The Second Sex* (1948) is a feminist treatise that was decades in advance of the major feminist movement of the late 1960s. Beauvoir was well known to be an atheist: certainly atheism was a basic assumption of Sartre's existentialism, but also of the marxist political philosophy which characterized so much of French intellectual life of the time and to which both Sartre and Beauvoir subscribed.

Simone, however, had not always been an atheist. She was born into a family of the high bourgeoisie, the elder of two daughters.[31] The family struggled financially as the money on both sides declined considerably over the years. Her father, a lawyer and to some extent a man about town, or boulevardier, was a skeptic, a definite unbeliever. Simone's mother was her major influence as a child and in adolescence. She was a very devout Catholic mother who brought up both of her daughters in a thoroughly orthodox Catholic manner. *In Memoirs of a Dutiful Daughter*, Simone describes herself in that period:

> I was very pious; I made my confession twice a month to Abbé Martin, received holy communion three times a week, and every morning read a chapter of *The Imitation of Christ*; between classes I would slip into the school chapel and, with my head in my hands, I would offer up lengthy prayers; often in the course of the day I would lift up my soul to my maker. . . . I madly adored Christ. As supplements to the Gospels, I had read disturbing novels of which he was the hero, and it was now with the eyes of a lover that I gazed upon his grave, tender, handsome face. . . . How comforting to know that He was there!"[32]

She considered becoming a Carmelite nun and appears to have been caught up in a romantic understanding of Catholic sanctity.

Simone was supervised with great diligence by her mother, who was in many obvious ways a most controlling person with respect to both of her daughters' lives. Madame de Beauvoir attended some of her daughter's classes until Simone was about ten, and opened and read her mail until Simone was eighteen.

By contrast, her father—like many fathers of the time—was dramatically less involved in the life of his daughters, but he was an important presence for Simone, who was quite aware of her father's attitude toward religion: "My father was not a believer; the great writers and the finest thinkers shared his scepticism; on the whole, it was generally the women who went to church; I began to find it paradoxical and upsetting that truth should be *their* privilege, when men, beyond all possible doubt, were their superiors."[33] Later, but still as a teenager, Simone lost her faith, becoming a skeptic or atheist: "My father's skepticism had prepared the way for me; I would not be embarking alone upon a hazardous adventure. I even felt great relief at finding myself released from the bonds of my sex and my childhood."[34]

Simone did not reveal her loss of faith to either parent at the time. It is perhaps not surprising that shortly after this, Simone discovered death—its great importance, and its troubling meaning. She also discovered loneliness: God was no longer with her. This sense of loneliness was in part mitigated by a few years of strongly emotional nature-worship, a sense of oneness with the natural world and its beauty.

Simone was about twenty when she met Sartre. They were both young students in Paris (Sartre was three years older than she), both studying philosophy. Simone soon became *completely* devoted to Sartre. She says in *The Prime of Life* (the second part of her autobioigraphy): "My trust in him was so complete that he supplied me with the sort of absolute unfailing security that I had once had from my parents, or from God."[35] Simone's devotion and loyalty to Jean-Paul lasted all her life—in spite of extraordinary disappointments in their relationship and considerable involvement on the part of each (especially Sartre) with other lovers. Throughout her life, in spite of her own affairs—some of them lesbian relationships— Simone showed wife–like loyalty to Sartre and to the ideas for which he stood.

How are we to account for her remarkable and unshakable allegiance to Sartre? One feminist, Tori Moi, asks plaintively, at the start of her biography of Beauvoir: "Why . . . does she seize every opportunity to declare herself intellectually inferior to Sartre?"[36] The answer to both questions is that Sartre became her God.

It is clear that she did not become an atheist because of a defective father. Indeed, her father paved the way for her to become an atheist. Hence, her case is not relevant to our understanding of the *origin* of atheism. But it does bear directly on *how* atheism is expressed differently in men and women *after* the rejection of God. Simone substituted her relationship with Jean-Paul for her relationship with God. She maintained a kind of ironclad devotion to this relationship which dated back to the foundation of her intellectual life. In contrast, Sartre put an explicit principle of atheism at the heart of his philosophy. With respect to relationships, Sartre is famous for saying "Hell is other people"; ironically, Simone's implicit answer was, "Heaven is the other person."

Ayn Rand (1905-1982)

Born in Russia into a well-to-do Jewish family almost destroyed by the Russian Revolution, Rand and her family emigrated to the United States in the 1920s. Here, she began her career as a philosopher and novelist, and is best known for her philosophical novels *The Fountainhead* and *Atlas Shrugged*, but she also wrote works on objectivist philosophy.

Her mother and father bore similarities to Simone de Beauvoir's parents. Ayn's mother, though less pious than Simone's, was the more religious parent. Her mother's

Jewishness was expressed in a social, emotional, and traditional fashion, while her father—with whom Ayn clearly identified—was skeptical, thoughtful, and an advocate of reason and individualism. From her childhood, Ayn actively disliked her mother and rejected her mother's values and social interests.[37] Her biographer, Barbara Branden, describes Ayn's discovery of her father's intellectual life and her relationship with him. When the family was still in Russia, Ayn (then known as Alice) and her father attended a political lecture. "The lecture was interesting but the conversation with her father afterwards was fascinating"[38]: "[Ayn] learned, for the first time, the extent of the intellectual sympathy between them in the realm of politics. . . . For the first time he was speaking to her as an adult; her ideas were to be taken seriously. . . . At last to her great happiness, she was receiving the sanction, the approval of her father. . . . It was the first time in the fifteen years of her life that she had loved and been loved in return."[39]

In fact, Ayn had an earlier love—a fictional hero. In the summer of 1914, when she was nine years old, she "read a story which she recognized, then and later, as a crucial turning point in her life."[40] The story, "The Mysterious Valley," was about English officers in India involved in an intense struggle with an evil rajah. Even years later, Ayn described the story's hero, Cyrus: "Cyrus was a *personal* inspiration, a concrete example of what one should be like, and what a man should be like. He was a man of action who was totally self-confident, and no one could stand in his way. . . . He helped me to concretize what I called 'my kind of man'. . . . Intelligence, independence, courage. The heroic man."[41]

Branden further discusses the importance of Cyrus by noting that he was the model of all of Ayn's fictional heroes: Howard Roark in *The Fountainhead* and John Galt and Hank Reardon in *Atlas Shrugged*. Branden summarizes the importance of this childhood hero for Rand's work: "It was not the stories in her novels, it was not the literary style, it was not the events that most accounted for the fame she was to achieve; it was the portrayal of the human potential: it was Cyrus."[42]

Despite her brilliance and her energy, Ayn termed herself an "anti-feminist."[43] For her, it was man, not woman, who represented the admired qualities of struggle, strength, and purpose. These were specifically masculine characteristics, and Ayn defined femininity as "hero worship" and she described herself, far into old age, as a "hero worshipper."[44]

With Ayn, as with Simone de Beauvoir, we see an ideal relationship taking the place of God, for it is clear that in important respects Ayn Rand, all her life, worshiped her idealized man, her Cyrus—indeed she reveled in the relationship. Rand also believed strongly in certain principles—but clearly they followed from her earlier love of them as embodied in her hero.

Jill Johnston (1929-)

Jill Johnston, a prominent feminist, was born in England, where she lived with her American mother for a few years before they moved to Long Island, New York. She was given to understand that her father had died, and she grew up an only child, living with her mother and maternal grandmother. There were no male figures present in the home. She was close to her mother, but was something of a tomboy as well. In 1947, she graduated from St. Mary's Academy in Peekskill, New York, a small private Anglican girls' school.

It was while she was in college in Boston that she learned, to her bewilderment, that her father had recently died. In other words, all the time her father had been alive and living in England; her mother had not been a widow after all. Since Jill had visited England as a child, this meant, of course, that she might have been able to know her father. Not only had her mother misrepresented the situation, but her father had never contacted her.

Jill continued to wonder about the relationship between her mother and father. She found out her parents had in fact never been married, and her mother had been keeping this a secret. In a confrontation with her mother, Jill called her a whore, and her mother called her a bastard.

Her *Autobiography in Search of a Father: Mother Bound* is a book with many references to the impact of the absence of her father, and to her mother's intense and tangled meaning for Jill. Johnston closes this book by saying that she came "into the world as a *fille de père inconnu* [daughter of unknown father]." She went abroad to discover what she could about her father, for she claimed that "only a father's daughter, or son, could function in a world governed by fathers."[45]

Johnston came to espouse what can be called the classic feminist religious position. In *Lesbian Nation*, an expression and celebration of the emerging feminist-lesbian network of the time, she observes "that religion in all its forms is the twin agent with the legal apparatus of governments to maintain the patriarchal orientation of society and as such to continue the repression of women by the various appeals to our 'higher natures' invoking the words and deeds of the exclusive male deity." She claims that "home, church and state are the enemies of sexual revolution." As many feminists do, she quotes Marx and, especially, Engels in seeing the family as a bourgeois and capitalist construction. The feminist analysis in many respects exchanges war between the sexes for the communist war between the social classes. In any case, the atheistic framework is clear. There is not, however, any special neopagan or goddess emphasis in Johnston's writings; her emphasis is on lesbian relationships as being of great importance for all women.[46] She had a most defective father—with results that are consistent with our present analysis.

Kate Millett (1934-)[47]

Kate was the middle of three daughters. She grew up in St. Paul, Minnesota, in a very Catholic family. As a child, she was deeply devout and identified especially with Jesus and his sufferings. She adored her father, who was a handsome, charming, almost romantic, figure. He was a construction engineer, involved in large construction projects and did a fair amount of traveling.

In 1947, when Kate was thirteen years old, this adored father suddenly abandoned the family and went off with a nineteen-year-old woman. There was no contact at all between their father and the family he left behind until 1962—fifteen years later—and even then the contact was very modest. After her father left the family, Kate told her sister, Mallory, that she would never let another man become really important for her.

Kate went to Catholic elementary school and to a small private Catholic girls high school. She then attended the University of Minnesota. During her years at UM, she was seduced by a lesbian professor of psychology. An outstanding student, she graduated from Minnesota in 1956 *magna cum laude*, Phi Beta Kappa, with a degree in English. She later studied at Oxford and the University of North Carolina and received her doctorate from Columbia University in 1969. Her doctoral thesis was soon published under the title *Sexual Politics*, a major feminist intellectual statement that put her on the United States cultural and political map almost instantly.

Her younger sister, Mallory, remembers Kate's going to her thesis defense certain that she would be rejected and torn apart by the entirely-male thesis committee. Instead, she passed with honors and was praised for her work.

In late summer, 1970, *Time* published an article on feminism that featured Kate, in which she claimed that her father beat her and her sisters.[48] (Mallory is dubious about this claim.) At the time *Sexual Politics* was published, Kate had been married for some years to a sculptor named Fumio Yoshimura. Nevertheless, in rather short order she became an active member of New York's feminist circles, which stood for lesbianism, witchcraft, and general neopagan religious ideas, with a strong political overlay of marxism. (Of course, she clearly and intensely rejected Christianity.) During this time, her marriage ended. Mallory remembers attending a Halloween party in the early 1970s. Shortly after she arrived, she saw Kate with a group of thirteen naked women sitting around a long table; each had, on the table in front of her, a very sharp knife and other objects including bowls of fruit and lengths of string. Mallory and a woman friend who was with her fled.

Kate Millett has been hospitalized at various points in the past two decades for mental disorders, and has been diagnosed as a manic-depressive. Her sister describes her as much involved in interpersonal power, filled with rage and anger, and often extremely unpredictable.

We can say that this is a clear example of a woman who, as a young girl, was abandoned by her father and was perhaps the victim of physical abuse as well. She later substituted for her original Christian and Catholic faith a belief in neopagan witchcraft and in the goddess, and an exclusive involvement in lesbian relationships—all within the framework of a feminist world view. Kate Millett now lives in rural New York state, where she runs a community for women artists.

EXCEPTIONS

Denis Diderot (1713-1784)

The reader might ask where in this book are certain other well-known atheists—or at least important intellectual enemies of religious belief. One important figure not yet discussed is Denis Diderot, one of the major figures of the French Enlightenment. He was certainly the most prominent public atheist of his time, better known than d'Holbach, for instance, because he had published many successful works. In particular, he was the moving force behind the French *Encyclopedia.*

Diderot and his father apparently had a positive relationship during Denis's early years up through his teens. Hence, Diderot is not an example that supports my hypothesis: he did not have a dead father or a father who abandoned or abused him. (Nevertheless, he was the author of the very Oedipal remark quoted by Freud and mentioned in chapter 1.)

A serious conflict with his father emerged, however, when Denis was a young man. He fell in love with and wanted to marry a woman of a lower class than his and of little culture or refinement. His father strongly disapproved of this choice and had Denis kidnapped and locked up to prevent the marriage. Denis escaped and did get married. The marriage turned out to be very unhappy as, indeed, the couple had little in common. At this time, his intellectual positions, in particular his atheism, became a source of estrangement between him and his strongly Catholic family. He and his father were never reconciled.

Though there is modest evidence for Diderot's hostility towards his father as a young man, in general my hypothesis cannot account for Diderot. It is, of course, possible that Diderot had some serious negative experiences as a boy, either with his father or with important father figures. Nevertheless, we can only base our judgment on the record as we have it.

However, quite different psychological factors may account for Diderot's position. Recently, Frank J. Sulloway, in *Born to Rebel*, has proposed that a person's birth order

in the family is a major determinant of later adult intellectual positions.[49] Sulloway presents a great deal of evidence to show that later-born children are very likely to
rebel against the established political or intellectual order. They are exceptionally open to new and radical ideas
that overturn the older views—whether the new idea is
as important as Darwin's concept of evolution, or as silly
as Gall's theory of phrenology (that character can be
determined by examining the shape of, and bumps on, the
skull). Sulloway does not discuss Diderot, but Diderot
fits Sulloway's thesis remarkably well. Diderot's first-born
elder brother became a priest and identified with his parents
and the established order. Diderot's views can therefore
be seen as a consequence of an early family-based psychology—but not of course as a good example of the
defective father hypothesis.

Karl Marx (1818-1883): A partial exception

Karl Marx, the intellectual father of marxism—and therefore of socialism and communism—was also a prominent
atheist, but did not spend much of his time fighting the
atheist battle. He understood God in Feuerbach's terms,
as a projection of man's own disguised idealization of
himself, and understood religion, like other social phe-
nomena, as an expression of the material structure of the
time. There is one interpretation that would allow us to
see Marx as an example of my hypothesis. Although Karl's
father came from a long line of Jewish rabbis, he converted to Protestant Christianity, primarily for social reasons. As a young man, Karl Marx showed some Christian
belief. No doubt, young Karl knew that his father's in-

volvement with Christianity was superficial and it is possible that this awareness diminished Karl's respect for his father. Nevertheless, there is no clear conflict or estrangement between the older Marx and Karl, although sometime in his late teens when he was away at the university, Karl suddenly and radically rejected his bourgeois background—though he continued to accept his father's financial support. (It was the 1840s, but it sounds like the 1960s). Hence, there is reason to believe that Marx's lack of respect for his father is involved in his great hostility to the bourgeois class, of which his own father was his first and primary representative. In any case, his communist theory can be said to be a violent attack on everything his father represented; his ideas, therefore, constitute a good *prima facie* case for his rejection of his father.

OTHER PSYCHOLOGIES OF UNBELIEF

Many people are aware of how particular experiences with representatives of God, Christianity, or the Church affect their religious belief. I knew of a man who had been an atheist for much of his life, but eventually came back to Christianity as a member of the Episcopal Church. He had left the Catholic Church and rejected God because of a particular painful experience: when he made his first communion, he accidentally dropped the host and was publicly chastised, indeed humiliated, by the priest. He felt that wound so deeply that he lost his faith. There are no doubt many examples of the behavior of those who supposedly represent God causing such wounds. It is important, however, to keep in mind that however natural and human such reactions are, they are not rational, but psychological.

Let us look at another psychological basis for turning away from God. The great English historian Edward Gibbon, famous for his *Decline and Fall of the Roman Empire*, is well known for his attacks on the Christian Church and his clear implication that the rise of Christianity was causally connected to the fall of Rome. He frequently, especially in his footnotes, makes critical remarks about the early Christian Church. Gibbon's own personal psychology has been discussed in some detail by his biographers. One major biographer, Joseph Ward Swain, in *Edward Gibbon the Historian*, points out that Gibbon had definite religious inclinations, and when he had just arrived at Oxford, suddenly converted to Roman Catholicism.[50] His father was shocked at this unexpected—not to mention socially and politically dangerous—conversion on the part of his son. (At the time, in English society, there was much anti-Catholic prejudice and many anti-Catholic laws were still on the books; in particular, a Catholic could not serve in Parliament—a future that Gibbon's father hoped for his son.) His father immediately sent young Edward to stay with a Protestant minister in Lausanne, Switzerland, for several years. Within a year of his arrival, under pressure from the minister and his father, Gibbon returned to the Protestantism of his family. In the long run, however, he became more or less a skeptic in the tradition of the eighteenth-century rationalists—and, as noted, a critic of Christianity.

Swain quotes a famous criticism of Gibbon: "[Gibbon] often makes, when he cannot readily find, an occasion to insult our religion, which he hates so cordially that he might seem to revenge some personal injury."[51] Swain goes on to remark, "as to the personal injury there can be no doubt: Gibbon's life had been disrupted for years by his conversion to Rome, and he carried the scars ever after. In attacking the Church, however, Gibbon was actuated not by a desire to avenge these sufferings, but by fear—fear that he might again do something impulsive if he let himself go." Swain sees Gibbon as reacting against the religious enthusiasm characteristic of some members of his family—and indeed of a side of Gibbon's own character:

> [Gibbon] trembled at the thought of giving way to religious emotions. He therefore disciplined himself rigorously, adopting a coldly rationalistic attitude towards life and building up the picture of Christianity that we find in his History. The general pattern of his anticlericalism therefore resembles that of his conduct towards Suzanne Curchod [the only woman with whom Gibbon appears ever to have been deeply in love] during his second stay at Lausanne; he knew that he could never marry her, much as he might desire it, but he found that he could not forget her or even keep away from her; he therefore accused her (falsely) of various delinquencies in order to convince himself that she was unworthy of him; but after she was safely married to M. Necker he quickly forgot her alleged shortcomings and gladly accepted her as a dear and lifelong friend. He put on the same defensive armour against the Church, though fortifying his denunciations with wit rather than with indignation: he never

made jokes at Suzanne's expense, and only rarely was
he really indignant with the early Christians.[52]

Along with Sulloway's birth-order hypothesis, we have
here two other kinds of motives for the rejection of God:
painful experiences with representatives of religion (as in
the first case discussed above), and painful struggles within
the self (as in the case of Gibbon).

OUR PRIMARY PSYCHOLOGICAL THESIS and the evidence
supporting it have assumed that the basic experience of
one's father as either positive or negative is a major contributor to belief or unbelief in God. It is, of course, altogether possible—perhaps even relatively common—that
the experience and internal representation of one's father
can consist of separated or split representations—one image
positive, the other negative. In such cases, a more complex relationship to God may develop. For example,
positive aspects of the internal representation can support belief in a loving God, while the negative aspects
might be represented by the devil or a negative view of
religious authorities such as the Pope, whom Catholics
call "the Holy Father." If these two conflicting representations are strong, then an intensely ambivalent religious
attitude might result. Something of this sort may occur
in the psychology of certain charismatic or revolutionary religious figures.

A psychologist colleague of mine who has worked with
many members of the Catholic clergy has described the
psychology of a number of priests whom he has seen in
a way that supports such an interpretation. These priests

have a strong attachment to Jesus, but a weak attachment to God—especially as God the Father. They also strongly reject—some even hate—the Pope. My colleague has said that in all these cases the psychological connection between the priests' distant and punitive father and their rejection of the Pope has been very clear. According to this psychiatrist, such a psychology is not rare even among bishops. This complex psychological interpretation, based on a split in internal father representations, remains to be fully studied and substantiated.

Hence, in spite of the effect of defective fathers, there are other important psychologies that also result in atheism or "atheist-like" mentalities. Some we have noted or suggested; others may be combinations or permutations of these psychologies.

5

Superficial Atheism: A Personal Account

NO PSYCHOLOGICAL CRITIQUE OF ATHEISM would be complete without an examiniation of its more shallow and much more common forms. Let me start with my own case history. After a rather wishy-washy Christian upbringing, I became an atheist in college (at the University of Michigan in the 1950s), and remained so throughout graduate school (at Stanford University) and my first years as a young experimental psychologist at New York University. I rediscovered Christianity in my late thirties in the very secular environment of academic psychology in New York City.

On reflection, I have seen that my reasons for becoming, and remaining, an atheist-skeptic from age eighteen to age thirty-eight were, on the whole, superficial and lacking in serious intellectual and moral foundation. Furthermore, I am convinced that these reasons are common among Americans, especially in intellectual, academic, and artistic communities and in the media.

As a student of psychology, I was supported in my atheism by various general ideas. The argument—criticized here—that God is a projection of psychological needs, particularly childish needs, was one that I accepted. Supporting this psychological interpretation was a cultural or anthropological critique of belief as such. I am not sure where I learned it, though I do remember enjoying a course at the University of Michigan taught by an outspokenly atheistic professor of anthropology.[1]

I also believed in "evolution," including the evolution of worldviews. It seemed to me that primitive man had gods, goddesses, and spirits of many types: in this animistic phase, deities inhabited many natural locales (springs, woods, impressive animals, large distinctive rocks, and the like). Somewhat more "advanced" cultures had fewer deities but were still polytheistic. By the time of the Greeks or the Egyptians, there was a relatively small number of gods and goddesses, with a fairly clear hierarchy; Judaism introduced monotheism as the natural conclusion of this progression from many to one. And of course the final answer for the "mature modern mind" was to do away with the divine altogether, to understand the whole process as a form of intellectual evolution or maturation. Thus, the evolution from many to few to one to none appeared to be both an historical and a logical progression.

Of course, I never seriously investigated the evidence for this view or questioned it in any way. It just seemed correct and obvious. If I had done my homework, even back then in the 1950s and 1960s, I would have found out that the "evolutionary" or "progressive" model simply does not fit the data and, if anything, should be reversed: that is, the evidence then and now supports the claim that the earliest humans were commonly monotheistic, since the religious beliefs of the most primitive tribes for which we have any information sustain this view.

Andrew Lang, years before Freud's religious theorizing, pointed out that highly primitive peoples such as the Australian aborigines had a religion with a High God or Supreme Being who was not a ghost of the dead or some lower deity raised to a higher power.[2] More recently, E.O. James, a distinguished scholar of early religion, has noted that Lang and, especially, Wilhelm Schmidt and his colleagues established that this kind of monotheistic High God is "a genuine feature of uncontaminated primitive religion" recurring among the most primitive people such as "the native tribes of Australia, the Fuegians in South America, the Californian tribes in North America and certain negritos and other negroids in Africa and elsewhere."[3] In general, these tribes are found in the most unsatisfactory environments, having been driven there by their more advanced neighbors—one sign of their primitiveness. These cultures are food-gatherers and have yet to develop the arts of agriculture; whatever hunting they do is very primitive.

Schmidt reported that "the name 'father' is applied to the supreme being in every single area of the primitive culture when he is addressed or appealed to. . . . We find it in the form 'father' simply, also in the individual form ('my father') and the collective ('our father')."[4] The name "creator" is also applied, but is not always found. A third common name for the supreme being is "sky god" or "sky lord." In addition, this figure is reliably seen as utterly righteous, his only response to anything morally bad is to abhor and punish it. The moral life of these primitive tribes is largely determined by their understanding of the morally good supreme being who is seen as the author of rewards and punishments.

Some ethnologists, like Schmidt, have claimed that *all* of the most primitive peoples of whom we have any knowledge exhibit some form of simple monotheism, though this point is debated.[5] For our purposes, we need only observe the undisputed finding, which is that many—perhaps most—of the most primitive peoples are monotheistic in the preceding sense. Hence, no evolutionary model which makes monotheism a relatively late development can be considered acceptable on empirical grounds. In fact, many of the commentators of different backgrounds who have observed the primitive monotheism of these simple people have noted its great similarity to Judaism, Christianity, and Islam in this regard.

Polytheism and the proliferation of deities seem to have begun when cultures or tribes met and blended, especially when one group conquered another. And by extension it would appear that as cultures turned into political empires, the number of divinities became still larger. We might call this the "Pantheon effect": make peace with a neighboring tribe or one you conquer by adding their important gods to your list.

From this perspective, religious historical change has generally been one of *devolution* or *regression,* in that cultures went from one god to a few gods to many gods—and finally, in the modern period, to every person a god. This is no doubt an over-simplification, but it looks closer to the truth than my original, sophomoric, model. Within this context, Judaism was a notable exception and can be understood as a return to the original state of simple monotheism—a state lost in more "advanced" cultures and from which the ancient Hebrews often fell. In fact, in the history of the Jews, we see many times how political, economic, and social relations with other cultures persistently undermined their monotheism by introducing new gods (such as Baal and Astarte). Again and again, in the face of social and political pressures, they had to return to monotheism in order to maintain their faith and cultural identity.

But the major factors involved in my becoming an atheist—though I was not really aware of them at the time—were not intellectual, but social and psychological. I turn to these since they are rarely discussed, even though there is good reason to believe that, at least for many people, social–psychological factors are far more influential than rational arguments.

GENERAL SOCIALIZATION

An important motivating factor in my youth was a significant social unease. I was somewhat embarrassed to be from the Midwest, for it seemed terribly dull, narrow, and provincial. There was certainly nothing romantic or impressive about being from Cincinnati, Ohio, and from a vague, mixed German-English-Swiss background—all terribly middle class! Furthermore, besides escape from a dull and, according to me, socially unworthy past, I wanted to take part, to be comfortable, in the new, glamorous secular world into which I was moving. I am sure that similar motives have strongly influenced countless upwardly mobile young people in the last two centuries.

Think of the Italian and Jewish ghettos that so many Americans have fled—or of the latest young *arriviste* in New York, mortified by his fundamentalist parents. The pressure from this kind of socialization has pushed many a young person away from belief in God and all that this belief symbolizes and entails.

I remember a small seminar in graduate school in which every member at some time expressed this kind of embarrassment and response to the pressures of socialization into "modern life." One student was trying to escape his Southern Baptist background, another a small-town Mormon childhood; yet a third was trying to distance himself emotionally and intellectually (as he had physically) from his Brooklyn Jewish ghetto. The fourth was myself.

SPECIFIC SOCIALIZATION

Another major reason for my becoming an atheist was that I desired to be accepted by the powerful and influential scientists in the field of psychology. In particular, I wanted to be accepted by my professors in graduate school. As a graduate student, I was thoroughly socialized by the specific "culture" of academic research psychology. My professors at Stanford University, however much they might disagree among themselves on psychological theory, were, as far as I could tell, united in two things: their intense career ambitions and their rejection of religion.

Just as I had learned how to dress like a college student by putting on the right clothes, I learned to think like a proper psychologist by putting on the right—that is, atheistic—ideas and attitudes. I wanted as few impediments to my professional career as it was possible to arrange.

PERSONAL INDEPENDENCE

Since the American War of Independence and the French Revolution, an exaggerated desire for independence has characterized much of Western society. To be a "self-made man," to be "autonomous" and "authentic," have been common ideals. A chip on the shoulder, "no-one-tells-me-what-to-do" mentality has been widely admired and has become a cliché of modern culture. Obviously, such attitudes fit especially well with the psychology of the young male. This kind of attitude easily generalizes into an independence from all restraint, and thus supports the rejection of belief in God. For me, as presumably for many, becoming an atheist was part of a personal infatuation with the "romance of the autonomous self."

PERSONAL CONVENIENCE

Finally, in this list of superficial but nonetheless strong non-rational pressures to become an atheist, I must list simple personal convenience. The fact is that, in the powerful secular and neopagan world of today, it is quite inconvenient to be a serious believer. I would have had to give up many pleasures (you may use your imagination) and was unwilling to do so. And besides, religion takes a good deal of time, not just Sunday mornings; the serious practice of any religion calls for much more than that. There are other church services, as well as time for prayer and Scripture reading, not to mention time for "good works" of various sorts. I was far too busy for such time-consuming activities.

ANOTHER EXEMPLARY CASE

One might think that the preceding concerns are restricted to particularly callow young men (such as I was in my twenties). But more mature persons of both sexes can think the same way. After all, if there is no God and only matter, if atheism is true, then there is no afterlife, no heaven or hell. As Dostoevsky observed, "If God is dead then everything is permitted." At a rather less elevated level, I took the message to be "Grab all the gusto you can!" For example, the atheist and materialist implications of Darwin's theory of evolution for our sexual behavior were one reason for its popularity. As Stanley Jaki has put it, "None other than Aldous Huxley singled out sexual license as the chief immediate benefit to be derived from agreeing with the *Origin* [*of Species*]."[6]

Mortimer Adler provides an exemplary case. A well-known American philosopher, writer, and intellectual, a professor for many years at the University of Chicago, he has spent much of his life thinking about God and religious subjects. In one of his books, *How to Think about God: A Guide for the Twentieth-Century Pagan* (1980), Adler strongly presses the argument for the existence of God, and by the latter chapters he is very close to accepting the living God. But ultimately he pulls back; he remains among "the vast company of the religiously uncommitted."[7] Adler leaves the impression that his problem is more one of will than of intellect. In his autobiography *Philosopher at Large* (1976), while exploring his reasons for twice stopping short of a full religious commitment, Adler admits that the answer "lies in the state of one's will, not in the state of one's mind."[8] He acknowledges that to become seriously religious "would require a radical change in my way of life, a basic alteration in the direction of day-to-day choices as well as in the ultimate objectives to be sought or hoped for," and he admits, "the simple truth of the matter is that I did not wish to live up to being a genuinely religious person."[9]

Here we have a mature philosopher's own clear statement that being seriously religious would be difficult, or at least too much trouble. In my own case, I now see that it was because of my social need to assimilate, my professional need to be accepted as part of the world of academic psychology, and my personal need for independence and an agreeable way of life that I chose to be an atheist. Hence, the intellectual basis for my atheism, like that of countless others, appears in retrospect to be much more of a shallow rationalization than an objective rationale.

6

Conclusions

A QUESTION THAT CAN EASILY BE RAISED with respect to our psychologically-based hypothesis is, where were all the atheists prior to the eighteenth century? After all, there have been plenty of defective fathers throughout history; and yet the rejection of God as a clear intellectual and ideological position emerged in Western culture only a few centuries ago. How does one account for this? Obviously, the interpersonal psychology of the family, though a major contributor to atheism, is far from a complete explanation of the phenomenon. There also must exist important cultural forces and supports before an explicit atheism can emerge. It is not that the psychology outlined in this book did not exist in earlier centuries, but it would have been expressed in a different way when the culture was not ripe for atheism. So the question is: how was the psychology of the defective father expressed before the emergence of systematic unbelief? Presumably there were many ways to express such a psychology; for example, hostility to and cynicism about fathers and authority figures, such as the King, God, and high-ranking churchmen. Many forms of satire and parody allow the expression of the same attitudes. Likewise, participation in revolts, rebellions, heresies, and many other social expressions of this underlying mentality have long been available.

Recently, much has been written about the absence of fathers in American families.[1] Presumably, this widespread defective fathering will cause an increase in contemporary skeptical attitudes towards God. But it may also result in an equally widespread "father hunger" which could manifest itself in a variety of ways, such as a growth in cults and support for political demagogues.

A related question might be: where are the great rejectors of God today? Why are there now so few intellectually prominent atheists? First, there *are* a good many important atheists today, but their message is hardly novel or dramatic. Rejecting God has little shock value, and so the culture is hardly aware of those who do. Indeed, in many respects, belief in God has become the more shocking and radical position—at least in the worlds of science, the arts, the media, and the universities.

INTELLIGENCE, AMBITION, AND WILL

In addition to cultural or historical factors, another necessary but not sufficient characteristic of the major public atheists is intellectual capacity. There is no doubt that all of the prominent atheists whom I have mentioned were also intellectually outstanding, and hence capable of mounting intelligent and often innovative intellectual critiques. Just as every great basketball player is tall, so all major atheists have been highly intelligent.

Another characteristic that seems to be found among major atheists is a significant level of ambition and, closely related to it, intellectual arrogance. To become a public figure in the intellectual world requires great ambition and energy; to hold an opinion contrary to that of the majority often calls for self-confidence of a kind that typically is based on or leads to arrogance. Many of our atheists have been characterized by their biographers as arrogant or ambitious. Voltaire is described as seldom trying to conceal his intellectual superiority. One of his teachers in the lycée (French high school) commented that he had never met a student "as much devoured by the thirst for celebrity."[2] Indeed, Voltaire's ambition and intellectual vanity are agreed upon by all his biographers. His passion was for fame; he was certainly not much motivated by love for others.

Feuerbach has been described as a lonely figure whose loneliness "was the product of an unsatisfied intellectual vanity."[3] Feuerbach considered himself a "philosopher of outstanding importance," an attitude that "rested firmly on the intellectual arrogance of the man."[4]

Nietzsche's pride and his arrogance, often to the point of pathos, are widely acknowledged. Indeed, his philosophy is a celebration of the will to power, of the superman, of the death of God. It is a well-sustained, violent attack on Christianity, often, very especially, Christ. Yet, besides thinking of himself as the Superman, Nietzsche also refers to himself as "the Crucified One"—hardly a sign of modesty. Sigmund Freud is often described by his biographers as ambitious, a trait best summarized in Freud's own statement about himself: "For I am actually not at all a man of science, not an observer, not an experimenter. . . . I am by temperament nothing but a *conquistador* (conqueror), an adventurer."[5] Freud's critics have frequently noted his ambition and his intellectual overconfidence; he often arrogantly rejected those who disagreed with him. Bertrand Russell's arrogance, intense hatreds, psychopathic coldness, and his frequent lies are discussed in a major recent biography by Ray Monk.[6]

Finally, there is a most important personal factor which is perhaps best described as *free will*. After all, the individual, whatever the cultural and personal pressures favoring or opposing atheism, must ultimately decide which way to go. At any given moment, or at least at many times, every person can choose to move toward or away from God.

The importance of will is exemplified in the following story about Adolf Hitler, reported by Albert Speer, Hitler's head architect. Speer said that only once before the collapse of the Third Reich did he ever see Hitler deeply disturbed. I quote the account as summarized by Benedict Groeschel:

> In 1935 the Führer had what was supposed to be a perfunctory meeting with the intransigent anti-Nazi Archibishop of Munich, Cardinal Faulhaber. The half-hour meeting lasted several hours and Hitler was badly shaken at the end of the interview. Considering the future career of the Cardinal, who was one of Hitler's most outspoken critics in Germany and a staunch defender of the Jews to the end, it is reasonable to assume that Faulhaber pointed out to Hitler the spiritual [and moral] implications of the

road he was on. Hitler never arrested Faulhaber for going so far as to have the Star of David with the yellow armband placed on the statues of Christ and Mary in the churches of his diocese.[7]

Despite this dramatic meeting, as is well known, Hitler did not change his anti-Jewish policies. But there is every reason to believe that in 1935 he still had a choice—enough of a choice to be shaken, and not just angry, after his meeting with Cardinal Faulhaber. As I noted earlier, Hitler had a highly defective father, but that is not the only factor accounting for his, or any person's, atheism. John Lukacs makes this point in his recent book, an historical reflection on Hitler.[8] Lukacs identifies Hitler's intense hatred as his dominant motive, a hatred that was almost certainly fed in large part by self-hatred. Lukacs also acknowledges several times that Hitler had been abused and humiliated as a child. Nevertheless, Lukacs makes it clear that Hitler was fully aware of what he was doing. Hitler *chose* to cultivate his hatred, not to resolve or repress it.

THE COMPLETE MODEL

Nietzsche, Marx, and Freud are famous as formulators of powerful theories, but these atheist masters do not bother to argue whether religious beliefs are true or false. Instead, they ask what motives would lead people to hold such beliefs. As we have seen, this mode of inquiry is equally applicable to them and their ideas. It is certainly time for such critical suspicion to be applied to the "atheistic" structures of government, law, media, and academia that have arisen in our time.

My ultimate interpretation of historically important atheists is that they are the product of their historical period, family psychology (that is, the defective father), intellectual intelligence and level of ambition, and—last but far from least—their own free choice. My focus, of course, has been on the family factors in the context of the defective father hypothesis.

The thrust of the atheist projection theory is that there is no God—only a psychological structure, representing God, created by each of us. This internal structure, moreover, is created out of our disguised selfish or narcissistic needs. This critique of belief is in its own way similar to the classic religious position represented by the First Commandment: "You shall have no other gods before me."

Idolatry is the worship of things made by ourselves. Originally, these were external things made with human hands. But idolatry also means worshiping internal psychological objects constructed from our psychological needs. The danger of loving a humanly-constructed God who satisfies our beliefs and desires has long been recognized by great religious writers. The life of spiritual maturity is often portrayed as a struggle against interpreting God in our own terms. The spiritual journey commonly requires the "refiner's fire," which is understood as the burning away of narcissistic representations of God. The very painful burning away of defenses, projections, and other "comforts" eventually permits a love of God in the absence of rewards for the self. This process can cause serious pain, as in the suffering of Job, the point of whose "test" was to show that even when all rewards were taken away from him he still loved God. In short, the psychological critique provided by atheism can be a valuable reminder and help to believers in their struggle to avoid worshipping a mere projection of the self—a kind of psychological idol.

Since *both* believers and nonbelievers in God have psychological reasons for their positions, one important conclusion is that in any debate as to the truth of the existence of God, psychology should be irrelevant. A genuine search for evidence supporting, or opposing, the existence of God should be based on the evidence and arguments found in philosophy, theology, science, history, and other relevant disciplines. It should also include an understanding of religious experience.

In one important sense, therefore, the present study is an argument in favor of the pre-modern idea that controversies should be settled on the basis of the evidence, not on the psychology of the interlocutors. In this framework, *ad hominem* arguments must be rejected as irrelevant—and psychological arguments are all *ad hominem*; that is, they address the person presenting the evidence and not the evidence itself.

On the other hand, in the actual, practical interaction between believers and unbelievers, the preceding study also supports a different conclusion. It seems clear from the kinds of evidence I have cited that many an intense personal "reason" lies behind the public rejection of God. If one wishes to genuinely reach such people, one must address their underlying psychology. Aside from the common, superficial reasons, most serious unbelievers are likely to have painful memories underlying their rationalization of atheism. Such interior wounds are not irrelevant and need to be fully appreciated and addressed by believers.

Some of the personal quality of the defective father psychology is captured in Russell Baker's autobiography.[9] Baker is the well-known journalist and humorist for the *New York Times*. When Baker was five years old, his father was suddenly taken to the hospital and died there. Russell, weeping, spoke to the family housekeeper, Bessie:

> For the first time I thought seriously about God. Between sobs I told Bessie that if God could do things like this to people, then God was hateful and I had no more use for Him.
>
> Bessie told me about the peace of Heaven and the joy of being among the angels and the happiness of my father who was already there. The argument failed to quiet my rage. "God loves us all just like his own children," Bessie said. "If God loves me, why did He make my father die?"
>
> Bessie said that I would understand someday, but she was only partly right. That afternoon, though I couldn't have phrased it this way then, I decided that God was a lot less interested in people than anybody in Morrisonville was willing to admit. That day I decided that God was not entirely to be trusted.
>
> After that I never cried again with any conviction, nor expected much of anyone's God except indifference, nor loved deeply without fear that it would cost me dearly in pain. At the age of five I had become a skeptic.[10]

Let us then conclude by noting that, however prevalent the willful choice of unbelief by an ambitious or arrogant intellectual, there still remain, in many instances, profound and disturbing sources of unbelief. It is easy to formulate the hypothesis of the defective father, but we must not forget or oversimplify the pain and the complex causes that lie behind individual cases. And for those whose atheism was conditioned by a father who rejected, or denied, or hated, or manipulated, or physically or sexually abused, or abandoned them, there must be understanding and compassion. Certainly, for children to be forced to hate their own father, or to be brought to a state of despair because of their father's weakness, is a tragedy. All children want to love their fathers—and to have fathers who love them in return.

Notes

Introduction

1. Alexis de Tocqueville, *Democracy in America*, trans. G. Lawrence, ed. J.P. Mayer (Garden City, New York: Doubleday Anchor, 1969), 291, 292, 293.

2. James Turner, *Without God, Without Creed: The Origins of Unbelief in America* (Johns Hopkins University Press, 1985), 44.

3. Ibid., chapters 5 and 6.

4. See, for example, *Religion in America. 50 years: 1935-1985.* The Gallup Report. Report No. 236, May 1985: Princeton, NJ, as well as more recent survey results.

5. Richard John Neuhaus, *The Naked Public Square* (Grand Rapids, Mich.: Eerdmans, 1984). Neuhaus continues to document and discuss the absence of religion from public life in his column "The Public Square" in the journal *First Things*.

6. There are similarities between modern atheism and certain ancient Greek philosophical positions which rejected the gods or at least assumed their irrelevance, e.g., stoicism, aspects of epicureanism, etc.

7. Sigmund Freud, *The Future of an Illusion* (New York: Norton, 1961) and *Civilization and its Discontents* (New York: Norton, 1961).

8. The first—short—published versions of the present thesis

were in P. C. Vitz, "The Psychology of Atheism," *Truth* 1 (1985): 29-36; P. C. Vitz, "The Psychology of Atheism: The Theory of the Defective Father," *Fidelity* 5:4 (1986): 29-36; and P. C. Vitz, "The Psychology of Atheism and Christian Spirituality," *Anthropotes.* 6:1 (1990): 89-106.

1 *Intense Atheism*

1. For those who reject free will (for example, materialists, some hyper-Calvinists), this book can be read as a thesis on the way that atheism is psychologically determined.

2. Besides the projection theory, there is another related interpretation of belief in God which Freud also developed, but although this has a very modest psychoanalytic character, it is also really an adaptation of the Feuerbachian position. This interpretation is Freud's neglected use of the ego ideal. The super-ego, including the ego ideal is the "heir of the Oedipus complex," representing a projection of an idealized father—and presumably of God the Father. See Sigmund Freud, *The Ego and the Id*, ed. and trans. J. Strachey (New York: Norton, 1962), 26-28, 38.

The difficulty here is that the ego ideal did not receive much attention or development within Freud's writings. Furthermore, it is easily interpreted as an adoption of Feuerbach's projection theory. Thus, we can conclude that psychoanalysis does not in actuality provide significant theoretical concepts for characterizing belief in God as neurotic. Freud either used Feuerbach's much older projection or illusion theory or incorporated Feuerbach in his notion of the ego ideal. Presumably this is the reason why Freud acknowledged to Pfister that his *Illusion* with its case for projection was not a true part of psychoanalysis.

3. Sigmund Freud, *The Future of an Illusion*, ed. and trans. J. Strachey (New York: Norton, 1961).

4. Ibid., 30.

5. Ludwig Feuerbach, *The Essence of Christianity,* ed. E.G. Waring and F. W. Strothemann (New York: Ungar, 1957).

6. H. Trosman, "Freud's Cultural Background" in J. Gedo and G. Pollock, eds., *Freud: The Fusion of Science and Humanism* (New York: International Universities Press, 1976), 47.

7. Feuerbach, 33, 11, and 49. Emphasis added.

8. Sigmund Freud and Oskar Pfister, *Psychoanalysis and Faith: The Letters of Sigmund Freud and Oskar Pfister*, ed. H. Meng and E. French, trans. E. Mosbacher (New York: Basic Books, 1962), 117.

9. P. Swales reports that one patient of Freud, a "Herr E," was a believing Catholic. If so, this is the only known example of such a patient. According to Swales, "Herr E" was important to Freud's development of the Oedipus complex. Of course, one patient hardly makes Freud an expert on religion—and this patient's history was never published. Swales discussed "Herr E" in an unpublished lecture, "Freud, his Ur-Patient, and Their Descent into Pre-History: The Role of 'Herr E' in the Conception of Psychoanalysis," National Psychological Association for Psychoanalysis, New York, New York, May 16, 1997.

10. For relevant research, see A.E. Bergin, "Religiosity and Mental Health: A Critical Reevaluation and Meta-analysis," *Professional Psychology: Research and Practice* 14:2 (1983): 170-84; D.B. Larson and S.S. Larson, "Religious Commitment and Health: Valuing the Relationship," *Second Opinion: Health, Faith & Ethics* 17:1 (1991): 26-40.

11. For a detailed development of this position, see P. C. Vitz and J. Gartner, "Christianity and Psychoanalysis, Part 1: Jesus as the Anti-Oedipus," *Journal of Psychology and Theology* 12 (1984): 4-14; Vitz and Gartner, "Christianity and Psychoanalysis, Part 2: Jesus as Transformer of the Super-ego," *Journal of Psychology and Theology*, 12 (1984): 82-90. See also P. C. Vitz, *Sigmund Freud's Christian Unconscious* (Grand Rapids, Mich.: Eerdmanns, 1993), chapters 4, 5.

12. Sigmund Freud, Standard Edition, vol. 17, (1919), 193.

13. Freud, *Totem and Taboo*, trans. J. Strachey (New York: Norton, 1950).

14. Ibid., 141.

15. Ibid.

16. Ibid., 142.

17. Ibid., 143.

18. Freud, *The Ego and the Id*, trans. J. Riviere, ed. J. Strachey (New York: Norton, 1960).

19. See B. Malinowski, *The Father in Primitive Psychology* (New York: Norton, 1927) and *Sex and Repression in Savage Society* (London: Routledge & Kegan Paul, 1927); W. Schmidt, *The Origin and Growth of Religion*, 2d ed., trans. H. J. Rose (London: Methuen, 1935); A. Kroeber and C. Kluckhohn, *Culture* (New York: Vintage, 1952); A.R. Radcliffe-Brown, *Structure and Function in Primitive Society* (London: Cohen & West, 1952).

20. Schmidt, 109-15.

21. Quite some time after developing this hypothesis, I came across the work of the philosopher John MacMurray who had similar thoughts along "Freudian" lines, when he wrote: "The wish to destroy the father and take his place is one of the common phantasies of childhood. Would it not be as good an argument as Freud' s, then, if we were to conclude that adult atheism was a projection upon the universe of this phantasy." J. MacMurray, *Persons in Relation* (Atlantic Highlands, NJ: Humanities Press, 1961), 155.

22. N. Torrey, "Voltaire," in P. Edwards, ed., *Encyclopedia of Philosophy*, vol. 8 (New York: Macmillan, 1967), 264-5.

23. O. Aldridge, *Voltaire and the Century of Light* (Princeton, NJ: Princeton University Press, 1975), 4.

24. Ibid., 28-33.

25. From *Rameau' s Nephew*, quoted by Freud in Lecture XXI of his Introductory Lectures. 1916-17, S.E. L, vol. 16, 338.

26. Freud, *Leonardo da Vinci* (New York: Vintage/Random House, 1947), 98.

27. For example, A.M. Rizzuto, *The Birth of the Living God* (Chicago: University of Chicago Press, 1979); J.W. Jones, *Contemporary Psychoanalysis and Religion* (New Haven, Conn.: Yale University Press, 1991); M. H. Spero, *Religious Objects as Psychological Structures* (Chicago: University of Chicago Press, 1992); W.W. Meissner, *Psychoanalysis and Religious Experience* (New Haven, Conn.: Yale University Press, 1984).

2 *Atheists and Their Fathers*

1. J. Bowlby, *Attachment* (New York: Basic Books, 1969), 256-57, 261; and J. Bowlby, *Separation* (New York: Basic Books, 1973), 34-5.

2. Friedrich Nietzsche, *Beyond Good and Evil*, trans. Walter Kaufmann (New York: Vintage, 1966), 13-14.

3. Nietzsche, *Ecce Homo*, trans. R. J. Hollingdale (London: Penguin, 1979), 51.

4. Ronald Hayman, *Nietzsche: A Critical Life* (New York: Oxford University Press, 1980), 17.

5. Ibid., 18.

6. Ibid., 17.

7. R. J. Hollingdale, *Nietzsche* (Baton Rouge: Louisiana State University Press, 1965), 10.

8. Hayman, 18.

9. Ibid., 26.

10. Nietzsche, *Selected letters of Friedrich Nietzsche*, ed. and trans. C. Middleton (Chicago: University of Chicago Press, 1969), 47.

11. Ibid., 300.

12. Nietzsche, *Ecce Homo*, 38.

13. See Hayman, 259, and J. Lavrin, Nietzsche: *A Biographical Introduction* (New York: Scribner, 1971), 51.

14. Nietzsche, *Ecce Homo*, 41.

15. G. Abraham, *Nietzsche* (New York: Haskell House, 1974), 22.

16. Nietzsche, *Ecce Homo*, 47.

17. Cited in Hayman, 18.

18. Middleton, 206.

19. See, for example, E. C. Mossner, *The Life of David Hume*, 2d ed. (Oxford: Clarendon Press, 1980), 7.

20. Ibid., 27.

21. Ibid., 32-34, 597. For a discussion of Hume's life-long intellectual concern with religion, see J. Noxon, "Hume's Concern with Religion" in K. Merrill and R. Shahan, eds., *David Hume: Many-Sided Genius* (Norman, Okla.: University of Oklahoma Press, 1976), 59-81.

22. His amiability is summed up in his being known as "le bon David." For a short discussion of his character, see E. C. Mossner, "Philosophy and Biography: The Case of David Hume," in Vere Chappell, ed., *Hume* (Notre Dame, Ind.: Notre Dame Univesity Press, 1968), 6-34.

23. D. MacNabb, "David Hume," in P. Edwards, ed., *The Encyclopedia of Philosophy*, vol. 4 (New York: McMillan and Free Press, 1967), 74.

24. Mossner, *Life of David Hume*, 26.

25. C. Moorehead, *Bertrand Russell: A Life* (New York: Viking, 1993), 8.

26. Ibid., 18.

27. Ibid., 22.

28. Ibid., 35.

29. K. Tart, *My Father, Bertrand Russell* (New York: Harcourt, Brace, Jovanovich, 1975), 183.

30. Ibid., p. 184.

31. Ibid.

32. Moorehead, 23.

33. Ibid., 24.

34. Ibid., 1 (written on Bertrand Russell's 80th birthday).

35. Tart, 46-7.

36. Ibid., 184.

37. J.-P. Sartre, *Existentialism*, trans. B. Frechtman, (New York: Philosophical Library, 1947), 58.

38. R. Hayman, *Sartre: A Life* (New York: Simon and Schuster, 1987), 31.

39. Ibid., 33.

40. Ibid., 40.

41. Ibid., 41.

42. Ibid., 43.

43. J.-P. Sartre, *Les Mots* (New York: Braziller, 1964), 20.

44. Hayman, *Sartre*, 358.

45. R. Harvey, *Search for a Father: Sartre. Paternity and the Question of Ethics* (Ann Arbor, Mich.: The University of Michigan Press, 1991).

46. Sartre, *Les Mots*, 19.

47. Harvey, 53. Emphasis in the original.

48. Ibid., 15.

49. Ibid., 128.

50. M. Lebesque, *Portrait of Camus* (New York: Herder & Herder, 1971), 11-12.

51. Albert Camus, *The First Man* (New York: Knopf, 1995).

52. Ibid., 136. See also P. McCarthy, *Camus* (New York: Random House, 1982), 11.

53. Rudiger Safranski, *Schopenhauer and the Wild Years of Philosophy*, trans. E. Osers (Cambridge, Mass.: Harvard University Press, 1990), 54.

54. W. P. Bridgwater, *Arthur Schopenhauer's English Schooling* (London: Routledge, 1988), 12.

55. Safranski, 16.

56. Ibid., 17, 16.

57. Ibid., 26.

58. Ibid., 55.

59. Ibid., 58.

60. R. S. Peters, *Hobbes* (London: Penguin, 1956), 13-14.

61. R. S. Peters, "Thomas Hobbes," in Edwards, *Encyclopedia of Philosophy*, vol. 4, 45.

62. A. P. Martinich, *The Two Gods of Leviathan* (Cambridge: Cambridge University Press, 1992), 56.

63. See P. Springbord, "Hobbes on Religion," in T. Sorell. ed., *The Cambridge Companion to Hobbes* (Cambridge: Cambridge University Press, 1996), 350.

64. A. Vartanian, "Jean Meslier," in Edwards, *Encyclopedia of Philosophy*, vol. 5, 283.

65. M. Dommanget, *Le cure Meslier: Athée, communiste et revolutionnaire sous Louis XIV* (Paris: Lettres Nouvelles, 1965), 51. The translations are by E. B. Vitz.

66. Ibid., 18.

67. Igor Shafarevich, *The Socialist Phenomenon* (New York: Harper and Row, 1980), 224.

68. Dommanget, 74-76.

69. Ibid., 76ff.

70. Ibid., 17ff.

71. Ibid. For his influence on Voltaire, see also A. Morehouse, *Voltaire and Jean Meslier*, New Haven, Conn.: Yale University Press, 1936).

72. Torrey, "Voltaire," 264-65.

73. J. Orieux, *Voltaire*, trans. B. Bray and H. Lane (Garden city, New York: Doubleday, 1979), 9-12.

74. A. D. Aldridge, *Voltaire and the Century of Light* (Princeton, New Jersey: Princeton University Press, 1975), 7, 4.

75. Ibid., 4.

76. Ibid.

77. A. J. Ayer, *Voltaire* (New York: Random House, 1986), 4.

78. Ibid., 7.

79. Ibid.

80. R. Grimsley, *Jean d'Alembert* (Oxford, Clarendon Press, 1963), chapter 1.

81. J. N. Pappas, "Jean le Rond d'Alembert," in Edwards, *Encyclopedia of Philosophy*, vol. 1, 68-69.

82. See Grimsley, 289.

83. A. Vartanian, "Paul-Henri Thiry, Baron d'Holbach," in Edwards, *Encyclopedia of Philosophy*, vol. 4, 49.

84. P. Navell, *Paul Thiry D'Holbach* (Paris: Gallimard, 1943), 13-14.

85. Ibid., 15.

86. A. C. Kors, *D'Holbach's Coterie* (Princeton, New Jersey: Princeton University Press, 1976), 158.

87. Ibid.

88. Ibid.

89. Ibid., chapters 1 and 2.

90. E. Kamenka, *The Philosophy of Ludwig Feuerbach* (New York: Praeger, 1979), 15.

91. Ibid., 20.

92. Ibid., 20-21

93. Iain Benson made a major contribution to this discussion of Samuel Butler.

94. Malcolm Muggeridge, *Earnest Atheist: A Study of Samuel Butler* (London: Eyre and Spottiswoode, 1936), 9-10, 16.

95. J. Sherwood Weber, "Afterword" in Samuel Butler, *The Way of All Flesh* (New York: Signet Classics, 1960), 380.

96. Samuel Butler, *The Way of All Flesh* (New York: Signet Classics, 1969)., 39.

97. Ibid., 202.

98. Ibid., 242.

99. See, for example, P. Roazen, *Freud and His Followers* (New York: Knopf, 1975), 37-38.

100. Ibid., 24-25.; see also E. Jones, *The Life and Work of Sigmund Freud*, vol. 1 (New York: Basic Books, 1953), 22.

101. See J. M. Masson, trans. and ed., *The Complete Letters of Sigmund Freud to Wilhelm Fleiss: 1887-1904* (Cambridge, Mass.: Belknap/Harvard University Press, 1985), 230-31, 264.

102. See Vitz, *Sigmund Freud's Christian Unconscious*, 34, and E. A. Grollman, *Judaism in Sigmund Freud's World* (New York: Bloch, 1965), 50.

103. Freud, *Leonardo da Vinci*, 98.

104. This section owes much to Iain Benson.

105. Margaret Drabble, ed., *The Oxford Companion to English Literature*, 5th ed. (Oxford: Oxford University Press, 1985), 1956.

106. Joy Davidman, who eventually married C. S. Lewis, attributed her acceptance of atheism—which she later abandonned—to reading Wells's book at the age of eight. See Lyle Dorset, *And God Came In* (New York: Macmillan, 1983), 12. G.K. Chesterton wrote one of his most highly regarded books partly in response to Wells. See Chesterton, *The Everlasting Man* (London: Hodder and Stoughton, 1925).

107. Michael Coren, *The Invisible Man: The Life and Liberties of H. G. Wells* (Toronto: Random House, 1993), 22.

108. H. G. Wells, *Experiment in Autobiography* (New York: Macmillan, 1934), 44-45.

109. Ibid., 52-53.

110. R. E. Sullivan, *John Toland and the Deist Controversy* (Cambridge, Mass.: Harvard University Press, 1982), 127.

111. Ibid., 2. Most biographical material is taken from 1-9.

112. J. Herrick, *Against the Faith: Essays on Deists, Skeptics and Atheists* (Buffalo, New York: Prometheus, 1988).

113. Ibid., 145.

114. Ibid., 150.

115. Ibid.

116. Ibid., 153.

117. W. J. Murray, *My Life Without God* (Nashville, Tenn.: Thomas Nelson, 1982), 7.

118. Ibid., 8.

119. Ibid., 11.

120. D. Wiener, *Albert Ellis: Passionate Skeptic* (New York: Praeger, 1988), 7.

121. Ibid., 12.

122. Ibid., 21.

123. Ibid., 41.

124. Ibid., 42.

3 *Theists and Their Fathers*

1. J. Steinmann, *Pascal*, trans. M. Turnell (New York: Harcourt, Brace & World, 1962), 8.

2. Information taken from the *Dictionary of National Biography* (hereafter, DNB), vol. 2 (1917), 348-56, and from Arthur A. Luce, *The Life of George Berkeley, Bishop of Clovue* (London: Thomas Nelson, 1949).

3. Luce, 26.

4. Ibid., 22.

5. Ibid.

6. Ibid., 24.

7. DNB, 2:352.

8. Ibid., 350.

9. Ibid, 353.

10. DNB, 3:518-24.

11. DNB, 16:879-82.

12. Ibid, 879.

13. Alexander Campbell Fraser, *Thomas Reid*, Famous Scots

Series (Edinburgh and London: Oliphant Anderson & Ferrier, 1898), 10.

14. Ibid., 34-35.

15. DNB, 16:881.

16. Ibid.

17. DNB, 3:345-65.

18. Robert H. Murray, *Edmund Burke, A Biography* (Oxford: Oxford University Press, 1931).

19. Ibid., 7.

20. Ibid., 4.

21. Ibid.

22. Edmund Burke, *Reflections on the Revolution in France*, ed. L.G. Mitchell (Oxford: Oxford University Press, 1993), 86.

23. Ibid., 90-91.

24. See Murray, chapter XI.

25. Mendelssohn's biographical information is taken from *The Jewish Encyclopedia*, vol. VIII, (New York: Funk and Wagnalls, 1925), 479ff, and from *The Encyclopedia Judaica*, vol. 2, (New York: Macmillan, 1971), 1328ff.

26. For the early impact of his father, see A. Altmann, *Moses Mendelssohn: A Biographical Study*, (University, Ala.: University of Alabama Press, 1963), 9.

27. DNB, 15:191-99.

28. Ibid., 191.

29. Ibid.

30. Ibid.,105.

31. J. Pollock, *Wilberforce* (London: Constable, 1977), 5.

32. O. Warner, *William Wilberforce and His Times* (London: Batsford, 1962), 24.

33. A. Maurois, *Chateaubriand*, trans. V. Fraser (New York: Harper & Brothers 1938), 24.

34. K. W. Clements, *Friedrich Schleiermacher: Pioneer of Modern Theology* (London: Collins, 1987), 15.

35. Ibid.

36. Ibid., 18.

37. J. Ker, *John Henry Newman: A Biography* (Oxford: Clarendon Press, 1988).

38. Ibid., 15

39. Ibid., 23.

40. J. P. Mayer, *Alexis de Tocqueville* (Gloucester, Mass.: Peter Smith, 1966), 17-18.

41. Ibid., 1.

42. Ibid., 3.

43. J. C. Hardwick, *Lawn Sleeves: A Short Life of Samuel Wilberforce* (Oxford: Basil Blackwell, 1933), 7.

44. A. R. Ashwell and R. G. Wilberforce, *Life of the Right Reverend Samuel Wilberforce* (New York: Dutton, 1883), 2.

45. Hardwick, 2.

46. Ibid.

47. Ibid., 3.

48. S. Meacham, *Lord Bishop: The Life of Samuel Wilberforce, 1805-1873* (Cambridge, Mass.: Harvard University Press, 1970), 7.

49. M. Chaning-Pearce, "Soren Kierkegaard," in Donald Attwater, ed., *Modern Christian Revolutionaries* (Freeport, NY: Books for Libraries Press, 1947), 3-85.

50. Ibid., 7.

51. Ibid., 9.

52. Ibid.

53. Ibid., 11.

54. Ibid.

55. M. Nedoncelle, *Baron Fredrich von Hügel*, trans. M. Vernon (London: Longmans, Green, 1937), 4.

56. Ibid., 5.

57. Ibid.

58. M. Ffinch, *G. K. Chesterton* (London: Weidenfeld & Nicolson, 1986), 8.

59. Ibid.

60. Ibid.

61. Ibid., 9

62. Joseph Pearce, *Wisdom and Innocence: A Life of G. K. Chesterton* (London: Hodder & Stoughton, 1996), 6.

63. Ffinch, 13.

64. Pearce, 4.

65. Alzina Stone Dale, *The Outline of Sanity: A Biography*

of G. K. Chesterton (Grand Rapids, Mich.: Eerdmanns, 1982), 12.

66. Michael Coran, *Gilbert: The Man Who Was G. K. Chesterton* (New York: Paragon House, 1990), 14.

67. G. K . Chesterton, *The Autobiography of G. K. Chesterton* (New York: Sheed & Ward, 1936), 22-23.

68. Albert Schweizer, *Memoirs of Childhood and Youth* (New York: Macmillan, 1931), 81.

69. Ibid., 61.

70. Ibid., 80-81.

71. M. Friedman, *Encounter on the Narrow Ridge: The Life of Martin Buber* (New York: Paragon House, 1991), 3.

72. Ibid., 4.

73. Ibid.

74. Ibid., 9

75. E. Busch, *Karl Barth: His Life from Letters and Autobiographical Texts*, trans. J. Bowden (Grand Rapids, Mich.: Eerdmans, 1994), 68. Other biographical information comes from this source as well.

76. M. Bosanquet, *The Life and Death of Dietrich Bonhoeffer* (New York: Harper and Row, 1968), 23.

77. Ibid., 21.

78. Ibid., 22.

79. Ibid., 45.

80. S.H. Dresner, *Heschel, The Man* (New York: Macmillan, 1985), 13.

81. Ibid., 23.

4 Extensions and Qualifications

1. L. von Matt and H. Bosco, *Don Bosco*, trans. J. Bennett (New York: Universe Books, 1965), 9-10.

2. Ibid., 28-29.

3. Ibid., 29.

4. Ibid., 27.

5. Ibid.

6. Ibid.

7. Much of the biographical information in this section comes from A.N. Wilson, *Hilaire Belloc* (New York: Atheneum, 1984)

8. Ibid., 9-10.

9. Ibid., 2.

10. Hilaire Belloc, *The Cruise of the Nona* (London: Constable, 1925), 54.

11. Much of this treatment of Walker Percy was contributed by Iain Benson.

12. Patrick H. Samway, *Walker Percy: A Life* (New York: Farras, Straus and Giroux, 1987).

13. Ibid., 34.

14. Ibid., 37.

15. Ibid., 38.

16. Ibid., 38-39.

17. Ibid., 49.

18. Ibid., 59.

19. Ibid., 120.

20. A. Bullock, *Hitler and Stalin: Parallel Lives* (New York: Knopf, 1992), 5.

21. E. E. Smith, *The Young Stalin* (New York: Farrar, Straus and Giroux, 1967), 24.

22. Bullock, 9.

23. A. Bullock, *Hitler: A Study in Tyranny* (New York: Harper Perennial, 1971), 4.

24. J. Toland, *Adolf Hitler* (Garden City, New York: Doubleday, 1976), 9.

25. Ibid., 12.

26. H. R. Trevor-Roper, "The Mind of Adolf Hitler," in *Hitler's Secret Conversations. 1941-1944* (New York: Farrar, Straus and Giroux, 1972), xxiv.

Hitler presented Mussolini with a copy of Nietzsche's works, with a signed dedication. Accompanying the volume was a letter from Marshall Kesselring: "The Führer will consider himself happy if this great work of German literature gives you a little pleasure, Duce, and if you will consider it as an expression of the Führer's special attachment to you." Larry Azar, *Philosophy and Ideology*, 2nd ed. (Dubuque: Kendall Hunt, 1983), 70.

27. J. B. Schneewind, "John Stuart Mill," in Edwards, *Encyclopedia of Philosophy*, 5:314.

28. Carol Gilligan, *In a Different Voice* (Cambridge, Mass.: Harvard University Press, 1982).

29. S. L. Archer, "Gender Differences in Identity Development: Issues of Process, Domain, and Timing," *Journal of Adolescence* 12 (1989): 117-38; N. Chodorow, *The Reproduction of Mothering* (Berkeley: University of California Press, 1983).

30. M. Hoffman, "Sex Differences in Empathy and Related Behaviors," *Psychological Bulletin* 89 (1977): 712-729.

31. C. Ascher, *Simone de Beauvoir* (Boston: Beacon Press, 1981), 12-13.

32. Simone de Beauvoir, *Memoirs of a Dutiful Daughter*, trans. J. Kirkup (Cleveland, Ohio: World Publishing, 1959), 77-78.

33. Ibid., 143.

34. Ibid., 145.

35. Quoted in Ascher, 25.

36. Tori Moi, *Simone de Beauvoir: The Making of an Intellectual Woman* (Oxford: Blackwell, 1994), 15.

37. Barbara Branden, *The Passion of Ayn Rand* (Garden City, New York: Doubleday, 1986), 4-5.

38. Ibid., 31.

39. Ibid.

40. Ibid.

41. Ibid., 13.

42. Ibid.

43. Ibid., 17.

44. Ibid., 18.

45. J. Johnston, *Mother Bound: Autobiography in Search of a Father* (New York: Knopf, 1983).

46. Johnston, *Lesbian Nation: The Feminist Solution* (New York: Simon and Schuster/Touchstone, 1973).

47. My information on Kate Millett, unless otherwise noted, comes from personal interviews with her younger sister, Mallory Millett Danaher, in December 1996.

48. *Time*, 31 Aug. 1970: 18.

49. F. Sulloway, *Born to Rebel: Birth Order: Family Dynamics and Creative Lives* (New York: Pantheon, 1996).

50. J. W. Swain, *Edward Gibbon the Historian* (London: Macmillan, 1966).

51. Ibid., 68.

52. Ibid., 68–9.

5 *Superficial Atheism: A Personal Account*

1. The professor was Leslie A. White. His book, used as a text in the class, was *The Science of Culture: A Study of Man and Civilization* (New York: Farrar, Straus, 1949). White's book is thoroughly atheistic but his lectures were even more so.

2. A. Lang, *The Making of Religion* (London: Longmans, Green, 1898).

3. E.O. James, *Prehistoric Religion: A Study in Prehistoric Archeology* (New York: Barnes & Noble, 1962), 206.

4. Wilhelm Schmidt, *The Origin and Growth of Religion*, 2nd ed., trans. H. J. Rose (London: Methuen, 1935), 267.

5. James, 296–99.

6. Stanley L. Jaki, *The Savior of Science* (Edinburgh: The Scottish Academic Press, 1990), 124; see also Aldous Huxley, *Ends and Means* (New York: Harper, 1937), 316.

7. W. E. Graddy, "The Uncrossed Bridge," *New Oxford Review* (June 1982): 23–24.

8. Mortimer Adler, *Philosopher at Large* (New York: Macmillan, 1977), 316.

9. Ibid. Adler eventually overcame his reluctance to believe: in the spring of 1984 he was baptized and received into the Episcopal Church. See *Chicago Tribune*, 29 April 1984, sec. 1, p. 3.

6 *Conclusions*

1. David Blankenhorn, *Fatherless America* (New York: Basic Books, 1995).

2. A. D. Aldridge, *Voltaire and the Century of Light*, 12.

3. Kamenka, *The Philosophy of Ludwig Feuerbach*, 155.

4. Ibid.

5. M. Schur, *Freud: Living and Dying* (New York: International Universities Press, 1972), 201.

6. R. Monk, *Bertrand Russell: The Spirit of Solitude, 1872-1921* (New York: Free Press, 1996).

7. B. J. Groeschel, *Spiritual Passages: The Psychology of Spiritual Development* (New York: Crossroads, 1983), 64-5.

8. J. Lukacs, *History* (New York: Knopf, 1997).

9. R. Baker, *Growing Up* (New York: Congdon and Weed, 1982).

10. Ibid., 61.

Index

A Note on the Author

Paul C. Vitz, a professor of psychology at New York University, was an atheist until his late thirties. He earned his bachelor's degree at the University of Michigan and his doctorate at Stanford. Professor Vitz is the author of *Psychology as Religion: The Cult of Self-Worship*, *Modern Art and Modern Science*, and *Sigmund Freud's Christian Unconscious*, as well as numerous articles in professional and popular journals. He and his wife, Evelyn Birge Vitz, also a professor at NYU, are raising their six children in a faculty apartment in Greenwich Village.

This book was designed and set into type

by Mitchell S. Muncy,

with cover art by Stephen J. Ott,

and printed and bound

by Quebecor Printing Book Press,

Brattleboro, Vermont.

The text face is Caslon,

designed by Carol Twombly,

based on faces cut by William Caslon, London, in the 1730s

and issued in digital form by Adobe Systems,

Mountain View, California, in 1989.

The paper is acid-free and is of archival quality.

 18